SO-ACW-688

33: Terrorism
in Latin America

THE WASHINGTON PAPERS
Volume IV

33: Terrorism in Latin America

Ernst Halperin

THE CENTER FOR STRATEGIC AND INTERNATIONAL STUDIES
Georgetown University, Washington, D.C.

SAGE PUBLICATIONS
Beverly Hills / London

Copyright © 1976 by
The Center for Strategic and International Studies
Georgetown University

Printed in the United States of America

All rights reserved. No part of this book may be reproduced
or utilized in any form or by any means, electronic or mechanical,
including photocopying, recording, or by any
information storage and retrieval system, without permission in writing
from the publisher.

For information address:

SAGE PUBLICATIONS, INC.
275 South Beverly Drive
Beverly Hills, California 90212

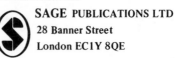

SAGE PUBLICATIONS LTD
28 Banner Street
London EC1Y 8QE

International Standard Book Number 0-8039-0648-X

Library of Congress Catalog Card No. 76-4103

SECOND PRINTING

---

*When citing a Washington Paper, please use the proper form. Remember to cite
the series title and include the paper number. One of the two following formats
can be adapted (depending on the style manual used):*

(1) HASSNER, P. (1973) "Europe in the Age of Negotiation." The Washington
Papers, I, 8. Beverly Hills and London: Sage Pubns.

OR

(2) Hassner, Pierre. 1973. *Europe in the Age of Negotiation.* The Washington
Papers, vol. 1, no. 8. Beverly Hills and London: Sage Publications.

CONTENTS

I. STRATEGY AND TACTICS

When terrorists rob a bank, hijack an airliner, kidnap an ambassador, assassinate a policeman, bomb a crowded restaurant, or murder an Olympic sports team, newspaper editorials and television commentators invariably maintain that such acts are counterproductive, since they turn public opinion against the perpetrators instead of winning sympathy for their cause.

Such comment is based on a misconception. As the word itself should indicate clearly enough, terrorism is effective not through inspiring sympathy, but through creating fear.

The terrorist seeks to demonstrate that his opponents are powerless to protect both themselves and the general public. He need not physically destroy his enemy; he needs only to destroy the enemy's authority or morale. Indeed, he may well win his victory not in the area of operations, where bombs explode and the assassin's bullets hit their mark, but in the distant capital of a colonial or protectorate power: in London or Washington, not in Dublin, Jerusalem, or Nicosia.

In Latin America, the Cuban terrorists who fought against the dictator Gerardo Machado in the late 1920s and early 1930s achieved their victory in this manner. The bombs exploding in Havana gave Washington the impression that the Machado regime was in a permanent crisis. It was only when President Roosevelt's decision to ease him out of office became known in Cuba that the internal opposition against Machado grew strong enough to overthrow him.

The present-day Latin American terrorists cannot and do not hope for foreign intervention on their behalf. Their aim is to bring about a revolution of the masses, and primarily of the working class. Their belief that determined action by a small group of revolutionaries can mobilize the masses is based on the experience of Fidel Castro's revolution. According to Che Guevara (1971b: 27), Castro's victory had shown that "it is not always necessary to wait until all the conditions for revolution are given; the insurrectionary nucleus can create them."

Castro's victory and subsequent defiance of the United States set off a long series of insurrections in various Latin American countries. Although as early as 1963 there was an ambitious, if short-lived, attempt at urban guerrilla warfare in Venezuela's capital, Caracas, the main emphasis in this first stage of the continental revolutionary campaign was on rural guerrilla war. However, the annihilation of the Peruvian guerrillas in 1965, the manifest lack of success of the guerrillas in Venezuela, Guatemala, and Colombia, and finally Guevara's own defeat and death in Bolivia in October 1967 cast serious doubt on his thesis: "In the underdeveloped Americas, the country-side must be the basic terrain for the armed struggle" (Guevara, 1971b: 27).

After Guevara's death the Latin American revolutionaries revised their strategy. The next insurrectionary movements, in Brazil, Uruguay, and Argentina, focused on the cities.

In Brazil, several urban guerrilla groups commenced operations early in 1968. The most spectacular feat of the guerrillas was the kidnapping of United States Ambassador Burke Elbrick in September 1969. However, the most prominent of the guerrilla leaders, Carlos Marighela, founder of the Acao Libertadora Nacional (ALN), was trapped and killed later that year. His successor as head of the ALN, Joaquim Camara Ferreira, was caught in October 1970; his death in prison became known shortly afterwards. Army Captain Carlos Lamarca, leader of the Vanguarda Popular Revolucionaria (VPR) was killed in September 1971. Mass arrests brought the urban guerrilla movement to a virtual standstill in 1972, although some terrorist activity continued in 1973. A Maoist rural guerrilla movement was still active in the Amazon in 1975.

In Uruguay, the socialist labor organizer Raúl Sendic founded the guerrilla movement that later assumed the name Movimiento de Liberación Nacional Tupamaros (MLN Tupamaros) as early as 1963. After years of preparation, the Tupamaros launched their large-scale guerrilla and terrorist campaign in 1968. The civilian authorities were unable to cope with guerrilla activities. In April 1972 the Uruguayan army assumed full responsibility for counterinsurgency operations, and within a year, the guerrilla movement was crushed. Sendic himself was wounded and captured in September 1972.

In Argentina, large-scale activities by several urban guerrilla groups began in 1970. One of the first major exploits of the guerrillas was the kidnapping and killing of ex-President Pedro Aramburu. Three successive military governments failed to crush the guerrilla groups, some of which were composed of followers of the exiled ex-President Juan Perón, while others were of Trotskyist or other Marxist inspiration. In April 1973 the military permitted free presidential elections, which resulted in the victory of the Peronist candidate, Héctor Cámpora. Perón himself returned to Argentina in June, and was elected president in September. The Trotskyist Ejército Revolucionario del Pueblo (ERP) continued its terrorist activities, notably kidnappings of foreign and Argentinian businessmen. The Perónist guerrilla groups were mainly concerned with the power struggle within Perón's ruling party, in which they acted as gunmen for the left wing against the conservative labor leaders backed by the president. After Perón's death and the assumption of the presidency by his widow in July 1974, the situation deteriorated still further. At this time of writing (December 1975) the ERP is conducting rural guerrilla operations in two northwestern provinces. The main Peronist guerrilla group, the Montoneros, has launched a series of attacks on military installations and personnel; their immediate aim appears to be to force a return to unpopular military rule.

Already before Guevara's death, the first theoretician of the Tupamaros, the Spanish anarchist Abraham Guillén, had challenged his doctrine by maintaining that "Today the epicenter of the revolutionary war must be in the great urban zones, where heavy artillery is not as efficient as in the countryside for annihilating guerrillas tied to the land" (in Hodges, 1973: 233).

The Brazilian Carlos Marighela still asserted (in Kohl and Litt, 1974: 83) that "The urban struggle acts as a complement to the rural struggle," but this was mere theory. In practice, Marighela's ALN, and the other Brazilian guerrilla groups waged their war in the cities.

Both Guillén and Marighela envisaged urban guerrilla warfare primarily as war against the armed forces of the state, the main form of combat being hit-and-run engagements of rapidly assembling and dispersing guerrilla units against army and police. Hence the apotheosis of the firearm in Marighela's *Minimanual:* "Experience has shown that the basic arm of the urban guerrilla is the light machine gun . . . The urban guerrilla's reason for existence, the basic condition in which he acts and survives, is to shoot" (Kohl and Litt, 1974: 95, 97).

This again was mere theory. In practice, the most frequent—and the only successful—actions of Marighela and the other Brazilian urban guerrillas were terrorist acts against civilians.

In the course of their struggle in Uruguay the Tupamaros developed views on the strategy and tactics of urban guerrilla warfare that were considerably more sophisticated than those of Marighela or of their own first mentor Guillén. A detailed Tupamaros pronouncement on urban guerrilla tactics published in 1971 specifically warns against premature confrontations with the police and military:

> Cold-blooded ambushing and killing at a time when violence is not yet at its height and the struggle has not yet taken on the dramatic character of a civil war, usually has effects contrary to those hoped for. The soldier and policeman feel that they are being attacked without provocation and react with indignation, moved by esprit de corps rather than loyalty to the regime [Tupamaros, 1971: 13-14].

Since one of the objectives is to draw elements of the armed forces over to their side, the authors of the document recommend an "indirect approach": to attack an object that is being guarded while sparing the guard; to surround a policeman and disarm him instead of killing him. "Revolutionary war is a political war" (Tupamaros, 1971: 13).

The document also warns against indiscriminate sabotage, which "generally is not accepted by the people with the same approbation as other revolutionary actions," (Tupamaros, 1971: 11) and should be reserved for the decisive, "dramatic" stage of the struggle:

> Even when the conflict has reached a certain height it may still be counterproductive to cut telephone, electricity, railroad lines, etc. . . . to the people these operations may appear as stupid sabotage without any strategic aim, and the government may in some cases appear as reestablishing a public service taken away by the guerrillas. Acceptable to the people are those acts of sabotage that only cause damage to the state or the armed forces or some capitalist . . . two more, secondary negative effects of sabotage are that it tends to reinforce the false image of "terrorist" which the government and the press wish to pin on the guerrilla . . . and that sabotage often cannot be exercised without imperiling adjacent zones (possibly buildings), thus creating fear of guerrilla actions among the population in general [Tupamaros, 1971: 11-12].

The use of time bombs in public places is condemned, because their explosion "can cause unnecessary victims among the population" (Tupamaros, 1971: 15-16). On the other hand, reprisals "for an act of injustice . . . such as torture, murder, an arbitrary court sentence, arbitrary dismissals by an employer or state official" are approved, albeit with the proviso that "the reprisal must be commensurate and adequate to the arbitrary action of the enemy which it is intended to punish. A disproportionate reprisal is also impolitic" (Tupamaros, 1971: 14-15).

It follows from this that bomb and bullet are to be used sparingly. The forms of guerrilla struggle most highly recommended in the document are

1. Kidnapping and revolutionary incarceration. Appropriate victims are "representatives of the regime, agents of repression, foreign representatives, and key personalities of the regime in general," also "recalcitrant employers during labor conflicts." Incarceration of kidnapped persons in "People's Prisons" or "Revolutionary Jails" is to be considered "one of the most effective means of confounding the plans of the regime," because of the enormous dispersion of manpower needed to guard every prominent person in his home and in the streets, and to search for the kidnap victims (Tupamaros, 1971: 16).

2. Requisitioning (Pertrechamiento). In urban guerrilla warfare this means, in the first place, bank robbery. "From the first moment of preparation for action, the guerrillas must plan the expropriation of great quantities of money, for money buys the 'Sierra Maestra' of the urban guerrilla, that is the hide-outs, also the workshops, the technical instruments and sometimes even the arms. Also they may plan the expropriation of strategic materials per se—such as machines, vehicles, and arms. The first requirement that must be strictly observed . . . is that only capitalists or the State may be expropriated, and in order to underline this, goods must be returned or damages compensated whenever the interests of workers are affected" (Tupamaros, 1971: 17).

3. Seizure of domiciles, that is, housebreaking and armed robbery of the apartments and mansions of "members of the agencies of repression, the government, the oligarchy, of imperialist foreigners, etc." This "carries the war to the peaceful and untouchable mansions of the personalities of the regime. The enemy is then obliged to disperse his forces in order to guard thousands of localities. The personalities of the regime are themselves constrained to a sort of clandestine life full of worries, and see their movements hampered by bodyguards even in their own homes" (Tupamaros, 1971: 17-18).

4. Armed propaganda. These tactics include seizure of radio and TV stations in order to broadcast proclamations, occupation of factories in order to harangue the workers, occupation of cine-mas, use of sound-wagons to play tapes while signs at the doors warn that they are boobytrapped, distribution of "expropriated" foodstuffs in the shanty-towns, and so forth. The document points out, however, that "the guerrilla band's fundamental means of expression is its armed actions," and that "generally, the best 'armed propaganda' is that generated by the big military actions" (Tupamaros, 1971: 18-19).

Actas Tupamaras, the volume authored by the Tupamaros from which the above declarations are quoted, also contains detailed accounts of 17 armed actions, a sample of the several hundred operations carried out between the founding year of 1963 and 1970. Only one of the 17 actions was aimed directly against the armed forces: the seizure of the naval training center in Montevideo in the early morning hours of May 29, 1970, by detachment of 22 Tupamaros. The training center was taken by surprise without a shot being fired. Sixty-three officers and men were taken prisoner and locked up in their quarters, and over 500 firearms and large quantities of ammunition, explosives, and tear gas grenades, as well as some radio transmitters and other equipment were seized.

The only other action that might be classified as military among the 17 operations listed in *Actas Tupamaras* was the most ambitious one in the history of the movement: the temporary occupation of public buildings in the town of Pando by a con-tingent of 49 Tupamaros on October 8, 1969, the second anniver-sary of Che Guevara's death. Two police officers and eight policemen were captured and locked up in the cells of the local police station, which had been taken by surprise, and the branch offices of three banks were robbed. As propaganda the operation was a resounding success, but the cost was heavy. During the retreat by truck and automobile part of the Tupamaro com-mando were cut off; in the ensuing shootout three Tupamaros were killed and 18 captured. The money robbed from the banks had to be dumped in a field and was recovered by the police.

The other 15 operations described in *Actas Tupamaras* were on a more modest scale: two seizures of arms in private armories, two bank robberies, two holdups of gambling casinos, one case of arson (the occupation and burning down of the General Motors offices and car park on June 20, 1969, in protest against the visit to Uruguay of Nelson Rockefeller), one kidnapping of a personality of the regime (Pereira Reverbel), one assassination of a police interrogator (Inspector Morán Charquero), the occupation of a radio station, one successful and one attempted liberation of prisoners from jail, the burglary of the main state-operated pawnshop in Montevideo, the burglary of a safe in the house of an oligarch, and the distribution of foodstuffs from a highjacked truck.

The *Actas Tupamaras* sample is not quite representative because it only lists operations through 1970, while Tupamaro activities reached their climax in the following year. It thus does not include one of the most spectacular Tupamaro successes: the escape of 106 members of the organization, including the leader Raúl Sendic, from Punta Carretas Prison on September 6, 1971. It also understates the frequency and impact of one specific type of small-scale terrorist operation—kidnapping.

In Brazil, Uruguay, and Argentina kidnapping has proved to be by far the most effective operation in urban guerrilla warfare. It does not require the deployment of large numbers of personnel: in fact, in the world of common crime it has often been perpetrated successfully by a single individual. Measured by the standard of economy of means, the number of participants habitually employed by the Tupamaros appears to have been excessive.[1] Unless the victim has surrounded himself with numerous bodyguards the operation, if well-prepared, is less risky than a bank robbery or even a common burglary. The difficulties come later, and only if a ransom has to be collected.

At the same time the psychological effect of kidnapping a person of any prominence is enormous: it gives the erroneous impression that the state, unable to protect its own servants or the accredited representatives of foreign countries, is pitted against an immensely powerful underground organization.

Besides seeking to destroy the military dictatorship's authority at home and its standing abroad, and to demonstrate that their main enemy was "Yankee imperialism"—of which the Brazilian government was allegedly a mere puppet—the Brazilian terrorists who kidnapped American Ambassador Burke Elbrick in September 1969 had an additional purpose: to obtain the release of imprisoned comrades. Ambassador Elbrick was released after the government had freed 15 political prisoners, who were flown out of the country; the government also agreed to the publication of a guerrilla manifesto by the censored Brazilian news media.

The Brazilian kidnappings continued. In March 1970, the Japanese consul in São Paulo, Nobuo Okuchi, was abducted and released in exchange for five imprisoned terrorists. In April, kidnap attempts against the U.S. consul in Porto Alegre and the German ambassador failed, but a second attempt to seize German Ambassador von Holleben succeeded in June. The terrorists exacted the release of 40 prisoners for his return. They then escalated their demands still further: 70 prisoners for Swiss Ambassador Giovanni Bucher, kidnapped in December 1970. This was the last kidnapping of the Brazilian urban guerrilla campaign. In the following two years, and possibly only for the time being, mass arrests and brutal counter-terror brought urban terrorist activity in Brazil to a virtual standstill.

Meanwhile, terrorists in other countries were following the Brazilian example. In 1970, Guatemalan terrorists kidnapped the German Ambassador, Count von Spreti, and murdered him when the government refused to meet their demands. The U.S. ambassador to Guatemala, Gordon Mein, was killed in an apparent kidnap attempt.

In Uruguay, the Tupamaros followed suit. On July 31, 1970, they kidnapped the Brazilian consul, Dias Gomide, and the USAID Public Safety Officer, Dan Mitrione. The kidnapping of the U.S. Embassy agricultural attaché, Claude Fly, followed a few days later.

When the Uruguayan and U.S. governments refused to negotiate, Mitrione was killed by his captors. The Tupamaros presented the murder of Mitrione as the execution of a death sentence passed by a revolutionary tribunal against a CIA and AID agent who had trained the police in "the art of mass repression and torture" (Kohl and Litt, 1974: 272). Nevertheless, the killing in cold blood of a helpless prisoner caused widespread revulsion in Uruguay, and a Tupamaro spokesman later admitted that "in this country an action which results in death has great disadvantages" (Kohl and Litt, 1974: 273).

Dias Gomide was released after seven months of incarceration on payment of a ransom of $250,000 raised by his wife. Claude Fly, at one time suspected of being the chief CIA officer for the Southern Cone countries of Latin America, was released without ransom in a state of poor health. British Ambassador Geoffrey Jackson, kidnapped in January 1971, was released in September after spending 244 days and nights in two successive "People's Prisons," hideouts situated in excavations underground.

Besides Fly, Jackson, and Dias Gomide, a number of Uraguayan government officials and businessmen were held in such underground burrows under the accusation of criminal activities, usually corruption. By this the Tupamaros sought to demonstrate that they were a "parallel power," implementing the law in competition with the Uruguayan state authorities.

In Leninist theory such a situation of "dual power" is one of the characteristics of revolution itself. However, for Lenin "dual power" was the *result* of a collapse of state authority. The Tupamaros, on the other hand, sought to install dual power in Uruguay during a phase in which the revolutionary movement still had to operate in secret. A Tupamaro spokesman claimed in 1970 that "it is becoming increasingly more clear . . . that there is a duality of power in this country. This duality of power is going to continue for a long time" (Kohl and Litt, 1974: 277). He was deluding himself. The existence of an armed clandestine group hiding kidnap victims in underground burrows cannot be compared to the open, albeit uneasy, coexistence of the official machinery of the Russian state and the new, revolutionary machinery of the Soviets during the revolutions of 1905 and 1917. It was this open coexistence that Lenin and Trotsky called duality of power. The proclamation of "dual power" by the Tupamaros is a characteristic example of the voluntarism of the Latin American New Left: they assume that a revolution can be brought into existence by declaring it to exist.[2]

In neighboring Argentina, terrorists linked with the left wing of the Peronist movement began operations with the assassination of trade union leader Augusto Vandor in June 1969. Terrorist activities by various competing groups were stepped up in 1970, the most sensational of their exploits being the abduction of ex-President Pedro Aramburu in May of that year. A few days after the kidnapping the terrorists announced that Aramburu had been sentenced to death by a "revolutionary tribunal," and that the sentence had been carried out.

In May 1971 the ERP (Ejército Revolucionario del Pueblo), a terrorist group of Trotskyist inspiration, initiated the long series of kidnappings of Argentinian and foreign businessmen for ransom. The first victim was Stanley Sylvester, manager of the Swift meatpacking plant in Rosario. Kidnappings in 1972 included those of Oberdán Sallustro, general manager of the Fiat motor company's Argentinian subsidiary, and of Ronald Grove of the Vestey corporation.

According to one source there were no less than 178 kidnappings of foreign and Argentinian businessmen in 1973 (Latin America, 1974). Among the victims were executives of such companies as Eastman Kodak, Standard Oil of Indiana, Exxon, Deltec, First National Bank of Boston, Firestone, Coca Cola, Swissair, and Peugeot. Ransom demands escalated. A mere $50,000 in food and clothing for the poor had been demanded and paid for the release of Stanley Sylvester in 1971. In May 1973 the Ford Motor Company paid $1 million to avert the threatened kidnapping of their Argentinian general manager by the ERP. The result was that three Ford executives and several bodyguards were killed later that year in kidnap attempts by other terrorist groups. In March 1974, Exxon paid the staggering sum of $14.2 million to the ERP for the release of its executive, Victor Samuelson, who had been kidnapped the preceding December. Even this payment was dwarfed in 1975 by the sum of $60 million reported to have been paid for the release of three executives of the Argentinian Bunge and Born concern who had been kidnapped in September 1974 by the Montoneros, the same leftist-Peronist group that had abducted and killed former President Aramburu in 1970.

The failure of three successive military junta governments to cope with terrorism was undoubtedly a major factor in President Alejandro Lanusse's decision to allow free presidential elections in March 1973. These were won by the Peronist candidate, Héctor Cámpora, who ordered the release of all imprisoned terrorists as soon as he had assumed office. The presence of Presidents Allende of Chile and Dórticos of Cuba at Cámpora's inauguration showed that the Latin American left held high hopes for the new Argentinian regime. The main Peronist terrorist groups declared their support for his government; the ERP, not linked to Peronism, refused to lay down arms. Former President Juan Perón returned to his country after 18 years of exile, and took over the presidency from Cámpora in September 1973.

Already under Campora internecine warfare had broken out between the left wing of the Peronist movement, which was supported by the terrorists, and the right wing, which was increasingly backed by Perón, and after his death on July 1, 1974, by his widow, President Isabela Martínez de Perón. In consequence, the terrorists returned to clandestine operations, the last to announce their formal break with the government being the Montoneros in September 1974.

As already stated, it is a peculiarity of urban guerrilla warfare that terrorist operations undertaken by a small number of personnel, and thus at relatively low cost and risk, are particularly effective. On the other hand, operations of a military nature, that is, direct confrontations with the armed forces, require numerous personnel, with considerable likelihood of failure, heavy casualties, and loss of prisoners who may be tortured into betraying vital secrets.

This obviously tends to pull the urban guerrillas away from high-risk military operations toward relatively less risky terrorist activities such as burglary, bankrobbery, kidnapping, and assassination of civilians or of individual military men separated from their units. But over the years, the propaganda yield of such operations diminishes, or rather turns sour. The terrorist is in danger of acquiring the image of a criminal rather than of a heroic soldier battling gun in hand for national liberation. Kidnapping for huge ransoms, in particular, can only be justified if the sums accumulated in this manner are used to provide the means for large-scale revolutionary actions. The guerrilla groups are thus forced to revert to a strategy of military confrontation.

A decision of this nature proved to be the undoing of the Tupamaros. They had hoped to move from terrorism to a higher phase in which the masses of the working class would join them in armed revolutionary struggle. The masses failed to respond. Thereupon the Tupamaros, with their characteristic voluntarism, arbitrarily declared the higher phase to have arrived. On December 30, 1971, they repeated their exploit at Pando by occupying the airport, radio station, and police station of the town of Paysandú. In their "Proclamation of Paysandú" they renounced the truce they had declared in order to participate in the presidential campaign of the Socialist-Communist Broad Front coalition, headed by General Liber Seregni, who was defeated in the election of November 1971. The proclamation claimed that the Uruguayan people were rising, and declared the government responsible for having "unleashed this civil war" (Kohl and Litt, 1974: 299).

Contrary to the teachings of Abraham Guillén, the Tupamaros also began to prepare for rural guerrilla warfare by digging underground hiding places in the countryside. Their name for these shelters was *tatuceras*—the word for the burrows of the large South American armadillo *(tatú)*.

On February 13, 1972, the Tupamaros assaulted the town of Socci. On April 14, they assassinated four persons whom they accused of being associated with "death squads" set up by the police: a former high-ranking government official, two police officers, and a navy captain. On the following day President Bordaberry declared a state of internal war, thereby handing over responsibility for counter-insurgency operations to the Uruguayan armed forces. Within a year and a half the Tupamaros were crushed. At this time (December 1975), it is impossible to assess whether efforts to rebuild the organization will be successful.

Uruguayan democracy was a casualty of the Tupamaro campaign. On June 27, 1973, President Bordaberry was pushed by the military into closing the Uruguayan Congress and Municipal Councils. He ordered the arrest of leaders of the congressional opposition and nominated a military-civilian council of state as executive authority, thereby becoming a puppet in the hands of the military leaders.

In the opinion of James Kohl and John Litt, authors of a standard American work on the Latin American urban guerrillas, the decisive factor in the defeat of the Tupamaros was the defection of one of their top leaders after a power struggle within the organization. Such power struggles are frequently symptoms of disorientation and demoralization.

Writing with an understandable lack of sympathy, a Uruguayan military intelligence officer, Colonel Sergio L. d'Oliveira (1973), attributes the defeat of the Tupamaros, inter alia, to "excessive intellectualism," which manifested itself in the "compulsion to write copious reports" and caused them to "drift slowly away from the national reality, to . . . separate them from the population," and to acquire an "inflated self-appraisal of the capabilities of the movement."

As further causes of the Tupamaro defeat, Colonel d'Oliveira mentions the military's "energetic and professional interrogation of Tupamaro prisoners"—a sinister phrase indeed—and the "incomprehensible" and "suicidal" decision to resort to rural guerrilla warfare. Of this he writes:

All the MLN doctrine up to 1971 agreed that the Uruguayan countryside was not appropriate for conducting guerrilla warfare. Still, Plan Tatú was designed to develop just that. In the absence of mountains and jungles to provide cover and concealment, the plan called for the digging of holes—where personnel could hide after an operation until the government's search efforts terminated. Underlying the plan was assumed logistical support from the cities, a supposed lack of rural antiguerrilla training on the part of the armed forces, and the self-appraised fighting capacity of the Tupamaros.

None of these premises proved correct. The cities abandoned the guerrillas. The army, made up principally of personnel born and raised in the country, adapted itself quickly to this type of combat. The city-born Tupamaros could not adapt themselves to living in holes with spells of hunger, cold, and heavy rains. Furthermore the army obtained ... the full cooperation of the local population which provided not only information, but transportation, and communication as well.

It was these operations that provided the leads which eventually spelled defeat for the MLN. The information obtained through interrogation of the first prisoners captured ... resulted in a chain reaction.

In Argentina in 1974, the terrorists of the ERP, hitherto the most experienced and successful of kidnappers, commenced rural guerrilla operations in the mountainous northwestern provinces of Tucumán and Catamarca. The ERP rural guerrilla nuclei are apparently still managing to maintain themselves.

The Montoneros, who acquired a formidable war-chest by the extortion of $60 million from the Bunge and Born concern, have launched a series of surprise attacks against military installations and personnel. The strategic aim appears to be nothing less than the total demoralization and subsequent disintegration of the Argentinian armed forces, which would leave power lying in the streets ready for the first-comer to pick up.

The Uruguayan experience was disastrous, but it would be risky to predict a similar outcome in Argentina. The Argentinian armed forces are discredited, and probably already suffering from some degree of demoralization, through the signal failure of the various military juntas that ruled the country in the 1960s and early 1970s. Furthermore, rampant inflation and spreading unemployment are radicalizing the urban and rural working class, driving even the most conservative labor leaders into opposition to the government of President Isabela Perón, and thus improving the guerrillas' prospects of strengthening their popular base.

II. SOCIAL ROOTS

A manifesto attributed to the nineteenth century Puerto Rican independence fighter, Ramón Betances, calls upon the people of the island to conspire against their Spanish overlords because:

> We lack any say and participation in public affairs; because, crushed by the weight of taxes which we did not decide, we see these flow into the hands of a number of incompetent Spanish bureaucrats and into the [Spanish] so-called National Treasury, while the sons of our soil, who are more worthy, occupy only some subordinate or unremunerated posts, and the Island lacks roads, schools and other means of intellectual and material development [quoted in Maldonado, 1971: 39].

These words were obviously not addressed to illiterate peasants and plantation-workers, but to educated persons, and in the first place to educated persons without independent means of subsistence and therefore in need of administrative employment. The Spanish civil servants, incompetent or able, have long been replaced, but to this day the program of Latin American nationalism remains the same: administrative positions for educated persons in need of employment, and social and economic development to create still more such positions.

The spread of secondary and higher education in Latin America has greatly increased the number of educated persons without independent means of subsistence and therefore in need of administrative employment. A completed secondary school education is the well-nigh indispensable prerequisite, though not the absolute guarantee, for membership in the upper sector—the *gente decente* (decent people) as opposed to the *gente comun* (common people)—of the two-sector social structure of Latin America. And a completed university education virtually guarantees acceptance into the ranks of the political and cultural elite.

Because of this, the influx into secondary schools and universities is determined by status considerations rather than by society's demand for graduates. Members of the upper sector, which includes the middle as well as the upper class, will make the greatest sacrifices to provide their children with an education appropriate to the status of the family, and will resort to ruthless pressure to push a reluctant or inadequately gifted child through school.

The lack of correlation between the influx of students and the demand for graduates creates the danger of widespread unemployment of educated persons and of the emergence of an "academic proletariat." In times of economic depression and stagnation, this can only be avoided by greatly expanding the sphere of responsibilities of the state in order to create new administrative positions. The educated classes have the political leverage needed to force such an expansion. The surplus of educated persons, the "academic proletariat," therefore does not actually emerge. Yet there is always, even in times of great prosperity, a potential surplus that does not show up in the statistics, but which manifests itself in a constant pressure to increase the opportunities for administrative employment.

For the economist, the endemic mass unemployment of manual labor that plagues the countries of the area is one of Latin America's most urgent problems, and rightly so. Unfortunately the Latin American politician usually has different priorities. His primary concern is to prevent unemployment in the upper sector, the educated classes, because 100 unemployed university graduates pose a greater threat to his position than 100,000 unemployed illiterates.

For reasons deeply rooted in the social structure and in the history of Latin America, the urban and rural working class of the area, the *gente comun,* only play the role of auxiliaries mobilized by members of the upper sector political elite to assist them in the interminable struggle for power, prestige, and above all, patronage. Only in Argentina, the most developed and in many respects the most European of all the Latin American countries, does the working class constitute an effective political force.

The political decisions in Latin America fall within the upper sector. The politically most active group within this sector is constituted by the educated persons without independent means and therefore in need of administrative employment. Decisions about patronage, the allocation of resources to the various government departments, the creation of new government agencies— in brief, control over the government—are of vital importance to them. That is why they provide the cadres for the political parties, the activists for electoral campaigns, the claques for political orators. And because of this, the primary concern of the Latin American politico is to satisfy them by providing administrative employment. As one Latin American political leader very frankly put it in a conversation with the present author in explaining his opposition to the military dictator of his country:

"Our country is poor, the state is by far the largest employer, *we have to take care of our friends,* and the President is not cooperating."

The complaints of nineteenth and early twentieth century travellers in Latin America about frustrating customs regulations and difficulties with passports, visas, internal travel permits, and registration and deregistration procedures indicate that already in those days the bureaucracy of the Latin American countries was seriously overstaffed, and was expanding its work-load in order to fill the available time.

At that time the bureaucracy was largely manned by younger sons and poorer relatives of the ruling agrarian, mining, and financial oligarchy. The problem of finding an occupation for the younger sons of the ruling elite is not specifically Latin American; it is probably as old as history. As can be seen from the biographies of such younger sons as Arthur Wellesley, Duke of Wellington, it could be a strong incentive to empire-building. In the countries of Latin America, which were too weak to embark on imperial conquest, the problem caused civil strife between coalitions of oligarchs seeking control of the state in order to dispense patronage to their clienteles—extended family, friends of the family, the families of friends. Caúdillos risen from the ranks of the illiterate soldiery were pampered by civilian leaders hoping to use them as tools; sometimes they turned against those who had sought to use them, establishing tyrannies in which members of the civilian elite were persecuted and humiliated. Dissident oligarchs turned to the urban lower classes, wooing them with radical phraseology in order to obtain a new power base. Scribes were hired to defend their masters' cause with the pen.

These scribes, often younger sons educated in Europe, used terms borrowed from the contemporary European scene to explain the issues to the reading public. The naked struggles for power were thus masked as conflicts of abstract principle: state versus church, federalism versus centralism, radicalism versus liberalism versus conservatism. One of the scribes, Venezuelan journalist Antonio Leocadio Guzman, cynically admitted after the great Federalist War that had racked his country from 1859 to 1863,

> I don't know where the notion comes from that the people of Venezuela are enamored of Federation, when they do not know what the word means. This idea originated with me and others who said to ourselves: since every revolution needs a flag, and since the Convention of Valencia refused to baptize the Constitution with the name Federal, let us invoke this idea; for if our opponents had said Federation, we would have said Centralism [Fortoul, 1947: III, 135-136].

The savage struggle in the upper sector continues to this day. The terminology in which it is masked has been modernized; today it is usually that of Marx, Lenin and his successors, or the

Catholic theorist Jacques Maritain. The real issue is still the same as in the nineteenth century: the conquest of the state in order to provide power and prestige for the leaders, and bureaucratic positions for their clienteles of educated persons in need of administrative employment.

In the first decades of the twentieth century the number of educated persons without independent means was growing rapidly. It now included numerous newcomers to the upper sector: persons of lower sector or immigrant origins. In the years of economic expansion many of them found employment in the private sector. Then came the collapse of the world market: the catastrophe of 1929.

There followed years of political turmoil. In most of the more advanced countries the old oligarchies were pushed from the rudder of the state by a new oligarchy of civilian or military politicians who came to power under the banner of populism.

In the Marxist interpretation, which has been accepted by many non-Marxist social theorists, Latin American populism was created and sponsored by a national bourgeoisie, a native Latin American entrepreneurial class opposed both to the landed oligarchy and to their alleged ally, "foreign imperialism." This thesis is untenable. The populist parties of Latin America came into being at a time when the entrepreneurial class of even the most advanced Latin American countries was much weaker and less developed than today; it hardly had a political will of its own, and was certainly in no position to enforce it. None of the founders of the populist parties was an entrepreneur, nor is there any evidence of massive support of the early populists by business. Indeed, such populist leaders as Rómulo Bétancourt and Haya de la Torre were originally regarded as dangerous communists by the domestic Latin American as well as the foreign business communities. With time, this changed.

One of the two main points of the populist program is nationalism, which in the Latin American context is practically synonymous with economic development. In the name of nationalism the populist governments have greatly increased the numbers and the financial strength of the entrepreneurial class by stamping import-substitution industries out of the ground: textile, durable consumer good, food processing, pharmaceutical, chemical, metallurgical, and engineering industries. In the words of the Brazilian economic historian Caio Prado (1966: 193) "there came into being around the state administration a dense network of private businesses directly or indirectly promoted by and maintained at the expense of the state."

One can thus say that if today there is a national bourgeoisie in Latin America, in the sense of a class of native entrepreneurs producing for the home market, it owes its existence to the nationalist development programs of the populist movements. The bourgeoisie did not exist when these programs were initiated, and therefore cannot have been their original promoter. It is the child, not the creator, of populism. And it remains dependent on the state, or more precisely, on the civilian or military politicians who control the state bureaucracy. This explains its inability to resist the implementation of the second main point of the Latin American populist program, although this point imposes heavy burdens on the private entrepreneur both as an employer and as a taxpayer.

This second main point of the populist program is social justice, which is to be brought about through labor legislation, the encouragement and direct sponsorship of labor unions by the state and populist parties, and through a complex structure of social security, health, and educational institutions. As a result, Latin American social legislation has come to rank with the most advanced in the world. In some respects it is more advanced than the social legislation of Sweden or Britain.

Since poverty cannot be legislated out of existence, much of the Latin American social legislation is unrealistic and has remained a dead letter or even become self-defeating. In most countries it has failed to improve the lot of the rural population, and the shanty-town subproletariat of the cities is only marginally affected. Nevertheless, skilled workers and employees in the more advanced countries of the area are protected in cases of accident, illness, or conflict with the employer; there are adequate overtime and vacation regulations, and pension funds are fed by heavy contributions from the employers.

This social legislation was not forced upon reluctant governments by a militant workers' movement, as had often happened in Europe. Even in Chile, where already in the 1930s there was an organized working-class movement of some numerical strength, this movement was not an independent force, and could only operate effectively as the junior partner in an alliance with parties of the middle class. Elsewhere the trade unions were pitiably weak; they only developed strength, and in some cases independence, through the good offices of populist parties and governments.

Indeed one can say that just as populism created the "national bourgeoisie," that is, the modern Latin American entrepreneurial class, it has also, and through the same process of import-substitution industrialization, created the modern Latin American industrial working class. What Leôncio Martins (1966: 188) writes of Brazil applies to most Latin American countries:

> When the present working class came into being, it encountered already in existence a body of social legislation guaranteed by the legislative authorities and a trade union structure guaranteed by the state.

We thus see that both the entrepreneurial class and the industrial working class were products, not sponsors and originators, of Latin American populism. To whom, then, did populism owe its tremendous dynamism?

To solve this puzzle one must ask if there is any other social group, besides entrepreneurs and industrial workers, which from the first profited by populist programs and continues to profit by them. The answer is obvious. There is such a group—the educated persons without independent means. In the years of depression, their clamor to be saved from proletarization by the creation of new administrative positions brought the populists to power.

The first main point of the populist program, nationalism (that is, state-sponsored economic development), calls for the creation of planning boards, new ministries and other government agencies, and parastatal enterprises, providing a myriad of new administrative positions from minister and director to janitor of an office building.

In a higher phase, nationalism leads to the confiscation of foreign enterprises, with or without compensation. This again creates numerous administrative positions, not only through the replacement of foreign employees, but also, and even more importantly, through the expansion of the administrative apparatus of the confiscated enterprises. Maximization of profits, the guiding principle of private enterprise, is replaced by a new principle: maximization of administrative employment opportunities. The demands of the administrative class—educated persons pressing for administrative employment—have precedence over the demands of the exchequer.

The implementation of the second main point of the populist program, social justice, besides adding a useful lower sector appendage to the populist clientele, again creates innumerable new administrative positions through the expansion of existing and the creation of new ministries and government agencies: social security agencies, health, education, welfare ministries, and above all, the Ministry of Labor. Through its arbitration courts and commissions, the Ministry of Labor implements the labor laws and settles conflicts; it thus obtains great influence over the labor unions, and in at least one country, Brazil, it exercises absolute control over them by collecting the union dues and portioning them out to the individual unions. It goes without saying that the intricacies of labor legislation and the complicated arbitration procedures also create employment for a considerable number of lawyers both on the employers' and on the unions' side.

Poverty cannot be administered out of existence, but in Latin America as elsewhere, the administration of poverty does provide employment for numerous sons and daughters of the educated classes.

The proliferation of bureaucratic positions represents a method of redistribution of national income: those in power apportion a larger share to those on whose support they depend. This has been denounced as parasitism, but such redistribution takes place in every society above the tribal level. A society in which each worker receives the full product of his labor, or is remunerated in proportion to his input, is a Lassallean or Saint-Simonian utopia.

The programs implemented by populist governments have considerably increased the number of those benefiting by this redistribution, while at the same time increasing the size of the cake to be distributed. The populist movements have forced social and economic change upon a rigidly hierarchical, innately conservative society. Change has been achieved through constant enlargement of the sphere of responsibility of the state. The force responsible for this is the administrative class—educated persons pressing for administrative employment. The administrative class, not the national bourgeoisie, let alone the proletariat or peasantry, is the single most dynamic stratum in Latin American political life.

The primary concern of the administrative class is the maintenance and perpetuation of its upper-sector status. This does not make the class conservative. Perpetuation means the passing on of upper sector status to the children of the administrative class. Since Latin American families are large, the demand for administrative posts is greater than the supply created by death and retirement. From year to year, the ranks of the educated persons seeking administrative employment are further augmented by children of the allied national bourgeoisie and of professionals: lawyers, doctors, architects, engineers, and academics. This engenders constant pressure for further social change, further extension of the area of responsibility of the state, from within the administrative class itself. For obvious reasons, the pressure manifests itself most openly in the places where the anxious supplicants for future administrative posts congregate—the universities and the upper grades of the secondary schools.

The extent and depth of Latin American student radicalism are in dispute. Quantitative studies by reputable sociologists show that even in universities that are notorious hotbeds of political extremism, the majority of the students participate only marginally, if at all, in political activities either in the university itself or in the public arena.

This merely confirms what every practitioner knows from personal experience: the majority is only drawn into action in rare moments of political crisis. Politics are made by a minority of trend-setting activists. However, some studies have uncovered a more surprising phenomenon: in the Latin American universities, the majority of students does not share the opinions of the radical trend-setters in whose domination of the universities it acquiesces. Thus, a study of university students in six Latin American countries, conducted by three American investigators in the middle and late 1960s (Liebman et al., 1972: 127), comes to the conclusion that "Actually, the Latin American student radicals represent only a minority of the students. The majority, indeed the vast majority, are either moderates or conservatives who eschew active participation in politics."

The authors of the study readily admit that their findings appear to be contradicted by the general leftward trend of Latin American university elections:

> Rightists and centrists constitute a majority among Latin American students, but they have been unable to translate their majority status into commensurate political influence. Throughout Latin America leftist students are a minority, yet leftists and their parties tend to win in student elections [Liebman et al., 1972: 130].

This is explained as follows,

> Student advocates of the right or the status quo are in a poor strategic position, especially in societies marked by extremes in living standards, racism, colonial exploitation and the like, to oppose, or rally support for an attack on, students who wrap themselves in the mantle of social concern and propose to do something about societal inequities. . . . The middle mass, lacking an ideological position to compete with the left, either moves to the left or becomes politically neutralized. In any case, it is the left which sets the political tone on the campus. In sum, the ideology of the left functions both as a shield for its adherents and as an impetus for action while the ideology of the right inhibits its adherents from acting on the basis of their beliefs or from building a mass base on the Latin American campus [Liebman et al., 1972: 133].

A Latin American student would have to be singularly thick-skinned to ignore that he is a member of a privileged minority. Many students are prevented by a sense of shame from openly supporting the status quo that protects their privileges. The same feeling impels others to demonstrate their social consciousness by activism in favor of an opposition party that proclaims the need for social change. Under a rightist government this will be the populist opposition. But when the populists are in power, they become the party of the status quo; however great their achievement, student activism is likely to swing farther left.

There is a further reason for the strength of the opposition parties in Latin American student politics: careerism. Students who are not well-connected face the prospect of beginning their careers near the bottom of a long and shaky ladder. Student activism is a means of establishing connections. When an opposition party comes to power, those students who have been the most active on its behalf are rewarded with high administrative posts. Unless parties already established in power are quite unusually dynamic, they have fewer such posts to dispense.

In Latin America, student politics is the best launching pad for a political career. The civilian political elite of Latin America is largely composed of former student activists. The Latin American politician begins his career in the university, or even earlier, in secondary school. It is there that he first makes a name for himself and assembles the clientele of friends and supporters that will accompany him through life. These clienteles, based on personal loyalty, account for the Latin American politician's remarkable staying power. Despite all the setbacks, the vicissitudes due to the inherent instability of the Latin American political system, there are relatively few instances of the meteoric rise, fall, and disappearance of political figures so common in the United States and in some European countries.

Well-connected students need not engage in university politics to further their careers. Yet some of them also join the ranks of the activists, impelled by youthful idealism, guilt feelings, oedipal resentments, sheer ambition, or a combination of such motives.

Under a democratic regime they have nothing to lose by radical activism. Family bonds being very strong in Latin America, their parents will forgive them once the time has come to settle down and find employment, or they may not even disapprove of the radicalism of their child. In times of political instability it is useful for the family to have a representative on the other side of the barricade.

Nevertheless, well-connected students generally have less incentive to engage in student politics even to the limited extent of voting in university elections. This doubtless explains the disparity between Latin American university election results, which usually yield a leftist majority, and the findings of sociological investigators, who perceive of leftism as a minority trend in the student body.

Matters are different when a government promotes such drastic social change as to threaten the very existence of the socioeconomic stratum from which the majority of the students are recruited. Then students who had hitherto been apathetic through inhibition or lack of political interest swing into action. The university is polarized into two irreconcilable camps reflecting the division in society, as happened in Chile under Allende and much earlier under Arbenz in Guatemala.

The proclaimed ideal of the student movement—a society based on social justice and free from corruption and patronage—is never attained. This has given rise to the notion that Latin American student politics are sterile and ineffective. The opposite is true.

As we have seen, the pressures for political and social change in Latin America are generated in the universities, rather than in the entrepreneurial class or the urban and rural working class. Nationalist foreign and domestic policies and the expansion of the welfare and labor bureaucracies are the political establishment's response to the need to provide administrative posts for educated persons in need of employment—a demand generated precisely by and in the institutions of education—the universities and secondary schools.

The pressure never ceases. It is somewhat alleviated by prosperity, which generates white-collar employment opportunities in the private sector. It is exacerbated by stagnation and depression. Then the student activists become intractable. They resort to violence, and find sympathy and support among the larger mass of their usually passive fellow-students.

Here lie the social roots of Latin American terrorism and guerrilla warfare.

III. SOCIAL ORIGINS OF TERRORISM IN URUGUAY, BRAZIL, AND ARGENTINA

The economy of Uruguay, the home of the Tupamaro (MLN Tupamaros, or Tupamaro National Liberation Movement) urban guerrilla movement, has been in a steady decline since the end of the Korean War. The country of some three million inhabitants is highly urbanized, with nearly half the population living in the metropolitan area of the capital, Montevideo. The literacy rate is well over 90 percent.

The populist policies initiated by the Liberal leader José Batlle y Ordoñez (1856-1929) have made Uruguay into a welfare state with free compulsory education, unemployment and health insurance, subsidized housing, liberal retirement benefits, and eligibility for a pension after 30 years of employment for men and 25 years for women. The agricultural wealth of Uruguay made it possible to implement these programs, whereas in other Latin American countries similar provisions remain on paper or benefit only a minority of the population.

The 1950s brought implementation of the other main point of the Latin American populist program: economic nationalism in the form of an import-substitution industrialization drive. However, the new industries that were set up were hampered by high payroll taxes and by the small size of the domestic market.

Agricultural production for the new processing industries was expanded at the expense of cattle pasture, causing a decline of meat production, the country's principal source of foreign exchange. One consequence of the import-substitution industrialization drive was rapid inflation. With the benefit of hindsight one can now see that the correct long-term policy would have been to expand the production of meat and grain crops for export, but at the time it was hardly possible to foresee the sudden rise of meat and grain prices on the world market in the 1970s.

The import-substitution industrialization drive was undertaken in response to strong pressures for the generation of new employment opportunities both in the private and the public sector. This resulted in a substantial increase both of the dependent and the independent middle class—paradoxically at a time when the per capita income and real living standard of the Uruguayans were progressively declining.

The numerical growth of the middle class was reflected in a spectacular rise in the number of secondary school students, which occurred in spite of a relatively low rate of population increase. Total enrollment in the schools of general secondary education, excluding vocational schools, rose from 36,700 in 1951 to 70,000 in 1960, to 90,000 in 1965, and to 123,000 in 1969 (UNESCO, 1973, 1963).

Total enrollment in the university also rose, though not to the same degree: from 11,700 in 1951 to 15,400 in 1960, to 18,600 in 1968 (UNESCO, 1973, 1963). In the same period the conditions of university study grew progressively more difficult as a result of the decline in living standards. Already in 1960 almost two-thirds of the male and over one-third of the female students in higher education were gainfully employed in the economy or administration, and in the overwhelming majority of cases this was fulltime employment seriously cutting down the time left for studies (Solari, 1968: 180).

The need to earn a living, the tightening up of requirements through the influence of professional organizations striving to slow down the increase in the number of graduates, and political unrest at the university all contributed to a prolongation of the period of studies. Thus, in 1963 the prescribed length of studies at the University of the Republic in Montevideo was six years in the faculties of law and medicine, and five years in the other faculties, yet the average age of the medical doctors who graduated in that year was 31, and the average length of their university studies was 12 years. The corresponding figures for lawyers were age 31, study-years 11.8; for notaries, age 28, study-years 8.2; for architects, age 28, study-years 9.5; for dentists, age 28, study-years 8.5; for economists, age 31, study-years 10.7; and for agronomists, age 30.5, study-years 8.5 (Solari, 1968: 153). It must be taken into account that the Uruguayan university is modeled on the continental European system and has no intermediate, bachelor's, or master's degrees.

An inevitable consequence of the lengthening of study years was a high dropout rate. On the basis of UNESCO data, and taking into account the length of studies and the increase in university enrollment, the dropout rate may be estimated at around 60 percent. Aldo Solari (1968: 151), the noted Uruguayan authority on the sociology of education, calculates an even higher rate of 72 percent.

The dropouts find their place in the social hierarchy between the elite with diplomas and the mere high school graduates. Solari (1968: 175) notes that, "very many law students, for instance, end up as bank employees in functions which are unrelated to, and offer no possibility of applying, the knowledge acquired at the university." The phenomenon is not restricted to Uruguay. Solari (1968: 38-39) states,

> In many Latin American countries incomplete university studies open the door to certain vocations which are hardly accessible to those who have only a completed secondary education. The phenomenon appears to be considerably more important than in developed societies. We can therefore imagine a scale at one end of which there is the concept that university education only makes sense as a complete cycle terminated with a diploma, and at the other end the notion of going to the university just for the time needed to find an

occupation. Probably intermediate and combined concepts will be the most frequent.

In Uruguay, with its highly developed system of state patronage, the university dropout need hardly fear actual unemployment, but he sees before him a drab white-collar existence with steadily declining real income. Many students and dropouts will already be witnessing precisely this in the homes of their parents. It is understandable that such an experience and such prospects may cause them to regard a total, revolutionary change of the social order as the only solution.

Students and dropouts thus became the most radicalized sector of Uruguayan society. In the aforementioned American study (Liebman et al., 1972: 129) of student orientations in six Latin American countries in the mid-1960s, Uruguay figures as the only country in which a majority of the students polled—a full 70 percent—had participated in two or more student strikes or demonstrations. Fifty-four percent of the Uruguayan students polled were favorable to the Cuban revolution, and only 37 percent perceived the effects of foreign capital as more good than bad (Liebman et al., 1972: 96). Over 50 percent were negative in evaluating professional opportunities, and only one-fifth believed that they would attain higher economic status than their parents (Liebman et al., 1972: 54). In another study dating from the same period (Van Aken, 1972: 55) it is stated that 80 percent of the students polled regarded the government as corrupt, and over 90 percent thought that it had allowed the country to slip into a deep crisis.

It is remarkable—and highly significant for the outcome of the Tupamaro guerrilla struggle—that the deterioration of living conditions did not produce the same degree of radicalization in the general public. In the Uruguayan presidential election of 1971, less than 20 percent of the voters chose the candidate of the united left—socialists, communists, Tupamaros. The great majority voted for various candidates of the moderate and conservative parties.

The first political base of Raúl Sendic, the founder of the

Tupamaro National Liberation Movement, had been a rural sugar workers' union, but the organization soon became totally urban and largely upper-sector, with students and white-collar workers as its main source of recruitment. In *Surviving the Long Night,* British Ambassador Geoffrey Jackson's fascinating account of his kidnapping and subsequent eight months of captivity in two Tupamaro "People's Prisons," the Ambassador relates that most of his captors—the periodically rotated prison guards and their superiors—were students with the sophisticated tastes of the highly educated Latin American. They provided their prisoner with good books: Cervantes and Shakespeare, Tolstoi and Thomas Mann, as well as the modern Latin American novelists. Besides the protest songs so beloved by young intellectuals, the taped music incessantly playing in their underground hideout included Bach, Vivaldi, and Beethoven. The one genuine proletarian among the guards, a factory worker, was soon replaced; Sir Geoffrey Jackson detected a failure of communication and a "trace of class-conscious disdain" in the attitude of his educated comrades toward him (Jackson, 1974: 184).

With the Latin American military man's characteristic dislike of oligarchs and intellectuals, Colonel Sergio D'Oliveira (1973) writes,

> The sociological and cultural background of the average Tupamaro places him in the same "bourgeois" and "oligarchic" class they fixed as their main enemy. This caused the Tupamaros to drift slowly into a theoretical stand further and further away from the national reality.

In a remarkably impartial study of the Tupamaro movement, Arturo Porzecanski (1973) gives data, compiled from press releases, on 648 Tupamaros captured or killed in action between December 1966 and June 1972. This represents the great majority of Tupamaros captured or killed during that period, but does not include some 4,000 Tupamaros and Tupamaro collaborators reportedly held by the military through the beginning of January 1973. Porzecanski's sample (1973: 28-29) includes information on the professions of 348 of the captured Tupamaros. Of these, 99 (29.5 percent) were secondary or university students; 109 (32.5 percent) were professionals or technicians; another 109 (32.5 percent) were workers or employees; and 19 (5.7 percent) had various other occupations. The category "professionals or technicians" comprises "anyone with a university degree or any-one likely to have completed a course of study at a trade or technical school" (such as nurses, priests, artists, mechanics, jour-nalists, and carpenters), while "others" include "housewives, soldiers, policemen, businessmen or land-owners, and the unemployed."

From what we have learned about the high dropout rate at the university we may justifiably conclude that a considerable number of the technicians and employees, as well as some of those listed as "others," had a background of uncompleted aca-demic studies. Since the difference between white-collar and blue-collar workers more or less coincides with the difference between the upper and lower sectors, or more specifically the middle and lower classes of Latin American society, it is regret-table that Porzecanski is unable to give a detailed breakdown of the category "workers or employees."

Porzecanski states (1973: 30-31) that "captured Tupamaros were usually in their mid-twenties, although the most frequently reported age was 21; however, one could have found guerrillas who were as young as 18 or as old as 59." He also finds that "the female participation ratio tended to grow from an original low of about 10 percent (1966-1969) to an average high of over 27 percent (1970, 1971, 1972)." Only 12 (1.8 percent) of the total sample were foreigners.

Porzecanski sums up his findings (1973: 31-32): "The Tupa-maros tended overwhelmingly to be Uruguayan, mostly in their twenties, with a considerable feminine membership, and a high proportion of educated people." As for the leadership: "an in-formal survey of the best-known and most important Tupamaros captured indicates that they tended to be in their thirties, were mostly male, and belonged overwhelmingly to the professional-technician group. In addition, they were all of Uruguayan origin."

Porzecanski (1973: 28) quotes a Tupamaro document which certifies that "the origin of comrades who were captured can be taken as a reference point" for the composition of the movement. He writes that he has not included data on the prisoners held by the military in 1972 because "the credibility of military sources in general has been severely questioned."

Yet the data (percentages only) given by Colonel d'Oliveira in his article in the *Military Review,* while more detailed, do not contradict Porzecanski's general findings, for as we shall see, specific contradictions in the data on the year 1972 turn out to be apparent rather than real, and the nature of the differences does not give one cause to suspect distortion for propagandistic reasons.

The colonel gives the following statistical breakdown of the "socio-cultural background" of the Tupamaros in 1969, which probably includes the prisoners taken in earlier years: 18.5 percent professionals with university degrees; 24.4 percent students (1.8 percent high school, 20 percent university, and 2.6 percent other students); 18.3 percent tradesmen; 26.9 percent employees; 8.7 percent bank clerks; and 5.2 percent workmen.

The colonel's data for 1969 indicate a movement in which university graduates and students—the country's present and future cultural and political elite—were heavily overrepresented, the dependent and independent middle classes—employees and small businessmen—were represented approximately in proportion to their percentage in the general population; while working class participation was practically negligible.

For 1972 the colonel (d'Oliveira, 1973) lists 8.1 percent titled professionals; 44.1 percent students (2.2 percent high school, 30.4 percent preparatory or similar, 11.5 percent university students); and 47.8 percent "employees, workmen in general." The most significant detail in the colonel's statistics for 1972 is the astonishingly high proportion of female Tupamaros. It had already been considerable in 1969: 39 percent. In 1972 it was 77 percent.

At first glance the colonel's statistic for 1972 would appear to indicate a marked change in the composition of the Tupamaro membership in the sense of a broadening of popular appeal as well as appeal to youth and even more to women.

The events of 1970-1972 do not bear out any such conclusion. The Tupamaros reached the height of their popularity in the course of 1970, but as they themselves admit, the murder of Mitrione in August of that year caused a setback. The marked decline in tourism, caused by terrorism in the 1970-1971 season, brought a further drop in the Tupamaros' popularity among the lower-sector population affected, and there is no evidence that subsequent events enabled them to rise again in popular esteem.

Nor do Porzecanski's figures for the period from 1969 to 1972 confirm the hypothesis of increasing Tupamaro appeal to the masses, youth, and women. There is a decline in the percentage of students of all categories from 38.9 percent to 20.1 percent and an increase in the professional-technician category from 22.2 percent to no less than 41.7 percent, while "the worker-employee figures fluctuated without any readily apparent trend." The mean age rose from 26.7 to 28.3, while the percentage of females reached its height in 1970 with 29.4 percent and sank to 26.2 percent in 1972 (Porzecanski, 1973: 29-31).

It must be borne in mind that Porzecanski's sample for 1972 only includes 325 Tupamaros whose death, capture, or conviction had been announced in the first half of the year. D'Oliveira's data, on the other hand, concern several thousand persons arrested in the course of the entire year. This leads us to a different explanation of the discrepancy between his figures for 1972 and his earlier figures, as well as those of Porzecanski.

Most of the Tupamaros included in Porzecanski's statistics and in Colonel d'Oliveira's statistics for 1969 were activists. But in the course of 1972, the military managed to reach and destroy the support organization of the Tupamaros, which had not been uncovered by previous investigations. It is precisely in the support organization that women and very youthful members were likely to be placed.

In an interview a Tupamaro spokesman asserted that "nothing makes men and women more equal than a .45 caliber pistol" (Kohl and Litt, 1974: 143). A chapter in *Actas Tupamaras*

(1971: 23) entitled "The Role of the Woman" states that "today [1970] almost all the action squads number a woman or two among their members," but the same chapter places more emphasis on the role of women in support activities such as liaison, caretaking in Tupamaro hideouts, logistics, and in "political work." In this last point, *Actas Tupamaras* betrays more than a trace of male chauvinism in listing as a specifically female contribution to "political work" the "feminine touch mentioned by Che in guerrilla warfare, be it in a carefully and competently prepared meal, be it in the fraternal gesture which alleviates the tensions produced by the struggle, be it in her continually human approach to those who surround her" (Tupamaros, 1971: 24).

The only plausible explanation for the astonishingly high percentage of women in the Tupamaro membership is that in contemporary Uruguay, women have even more reason to despair than men. In a male-dominated society they are seriously disadvantaged in the quest for employment in administration or in prestigious business establishments such as banks. They are expected to marry, but the declining economy makes marriage ever more problematical, and in marriage, the difficulties of establishing and maintaining a household are frequently insurmountable.

Statistics on the social composition of the urban guerrilla movement in Brazil are not available, but newspaper reports on arrests and on the release of captured guerillas in exchange for foreign diplomats indicate that it was similar to that of the Tupamaros. A public statement by a representative of one of the guerrilla groups, the *Movimento Revolucionario do Outobro 8*, reveals its social base: the young of the administrative class. In reply to the question "Where are the new recruits coming from?" he stated (quoted in Kohl and Litt, 1974: 143):

> With few exceptions, the members are under 30, some as young as 16. There are many students from sociology, the letters and arts, and law, fields with few prospects on the job market. We are beginning to attract a few workers.

However, conditions in Brazil differed greatly from those in Uruguay. The Brazilian urban guerrilla movements operated at a time when the economic and educational policies of the military dictatorship were beginning to pay off. The rate of economic growth was accelerating to 10 percent. Enrollment in the secondary schools of general education skyrocketed, but not in a situation of economic decline as in Uruguay in the 1950s and early 1960s. It rose from 750,000 in 1965 to 1,516,000 in 1970 and 1,734,000 in 1971. Enrollment in the universities rose from 155,000 in 1965 to 274,000 in 1970 and 321,000 in 1971 (UNESCO, 1973).

In consequence, employment prospects for educated persons in the economy, in administration, teaching, and allied professions were rapidly improving—even for students of sociology, the letters and arts, and laws. The natural recruitment base of the urban guerrilla movements in the administrative class shrank. This goes far to explain the fragmentation, the infighting, the doctrinal disputes, the frequent tactical shifts in the Brazilian movement— all symptoms of isolation and demoralization.

In Argentina the guerrilla movement is also split into competing groups, but their disputes lack the bitterness of the Brazilian squabbles. The economic and political conditions favor the movement. Argentina is a wealthier and far larger country than Uruguay, but the economic conditions are as bad, and the political conditions even worse. There is stagnation combined with rampant inflation, and political chaos is threatening to bring about the total disintegration of state authority. Already in 1960 the dropout rate from the universities was very high, second only to that in Uruguay (Solari, 1968: 138). The main recruitment base of the guerrilla movement still appears to be the same as it was in Uruguay and Brazil, yet there is a difference.

In Argentina there are definite links between the guerrillas and a militant working class, an alliance with the left wing of the Peronista labor movement which was established in the years of joint struggle against the military regimes. Of all the components of the Latin American New Left, the Argentinian guerrilla movement appears to be the only one with reasonable prospects of acquiring a mass base.

The political instability—the frequency of military coups in

Latin America—is often attributed to a particular proclivity for violence in the character of its inhabitants. The assumption is unwarranted. A highly competent quantitative study (Kirkpatrick, 1971: 201) of Argentinian political attitudes in the mid-1960s, based on an unusually large sample of 2,014 interviews, comes to the following conclusion:

"The single procedural aspect of political life on which there was general consensus was the undesirability of using force and violence to resolve political questions."

Another study (Fernandez, 1970: 93), restricted to the political elite, notes that "Despite Argentina's staggering record of coups and concurrent suspensions of basic freedoms, there is little evidence to substantiate the institutionalization of violence as a social value in the political life of the country."

After the factional strife in nineteenth century Uruguay, so impressively depicted in W. H. Hudson's *The Purple Land,* that country enjoyed constitutional rule unmarred by violence, interrupted only by a single bloodless coup staged by an incumbent president, from 1904 into the 1960s; during this period it became known as "the Switzerland of South America."

In Brazil, violence has been endemic for centuries in the northeast. Yet the Brazilian terrorists we have discussed did not pick this region as their base. The big cities of the center and center-south, Rio de Janeiro and São Paulo, constituted the main theater of their operations; but even at the height of the terrorist campaign, these cities remained safer for both inhabitants and tourists than New York or Washington.

More blood has flowed in Mexico than in any other Latin American country. Yet a particularly astute American observer (Foster, 1924: 181) who traveled extensively in Mexico in 1919, a year in which the savage turmoil of that country's great revolution had not yet abated, was "amazed to discover that the Mexicans do not appear a cut-throat lot." On the contrary: "The great masses of Indian and semi-Indian population appear quiet, simple, peaceable folk." [3]

The contemporary urban and rural guerrilla activities do not signify that the Latin Americans in general, or the Argentinians,

Uruguayans, and Brazilians in particular, are more inclined to violence than the inhabitants of Europe or the United States. Yet one cannot dispute that the individual terrorists tend to be people with an unusual inclination to violence.

Sir Geoffrey Jackson (1974: 162) describes his Tupamaro captors as being, with few exceptions, typical young Uruguayans of the educated classes, normal and average in every respect except one: they were more violent. Since their heads were always hidden in hoods, he could not see the expression of their faces. Yet,

> One of my profoundest sorrows has been the experience that, thanks to the discipline of the hood, I learned to read much from the human eye alone and now, without the hood, to recognize the eye of violence in the streets, shops, parks, even on the television screens of my own and other ostensibly terrorist-free countries.

Sir Geoffrey also registers the process of natural selection that eliminates from the ranks of the activists those who are unfit either because they cannot control their urge to violence or because that urge is not strong enough to overcome more humane emotions. On one occasion, one of his guards pulled a gun on a comrade during an argument, and was quickly removed to be sent to a Tupamaro court-martial. On another, a new female guard was seized by fits of sobbing at the sight of the "People's prisoners" cooped up in their narrow underground cages. She was taken away as being "temperamentally unsuited to the clandestinity" (Jackson, 1974: 168).

There are persons with an unusual tendency to violence in every society. In stable conditions they remain isolated even if they manage to present themselves as guided by the highest ideals. In conditions of widespread frustration they find supporters who, although themselves not addicted to violence, have concluded that violence is the only way to achieve a change for the better.

IV. IDEOLOGY

The Latin American terrorist groups are overwhelmingly recruited from the upper and middle classes, and they find
their main base of support in the universities and secondary
schools.

Yet these groups all claim to represent "the people" in its
struggle against domestic and foreign oppressors and exploiters—
the term "the people" *(el pueblo, o povo)* being synonymous in
Latin American usage with "the humble," "the common man,"
that is, the peasants and workers, the lower sector of the two-
sector Latin American social pyramid. This is no mere tactic, no
conscious deception perpetrated in order to hide their real aim—
political power and high administrative posts. It is a sincere belief,
for which they will brave torture and death. One could not
imagine a more striking confirmation of Karl Marx's definition of
ideology as false consciousness.

False consciousness cannot produce courage or intelligence
where there is none, but it can inspire naturally brave men to
great deeds of heroism, and intelligent men to the most brilliant
mental acrobatics. This is demonstrated by the life story of the
most celebrated hero of the Latin American New Left.

The Argentinian intellectual, Dr. Ernesto "Che" Guevara, joined
Fidel Castro's little band in order to fight for the liberation of a

small Latin American country from a brutal dictatorship. He hoped that this would be the first step toward the liberation of all Latin America from the yoke of imperialism and toward the construction of a new social order without exploitation of man by man.

In two years of armed struggle in Cuba, Guevara distinguished himself by unflinching, reckless courage, rose to the command of a guerrilla column, and directed the final, decisive engagement of the war—the Battle of Santa Clara. He was rewarded with two high administrative posts that he had never sought and for which he was hardly fitted by training or inclination: first the Directorship of the Cuban National Bank, and then the Ministry of Industries. He had thus inadvertently become a leader of the new Cuban administrative ruling class.

As Minister of Industries, Che faithfully promoted the interests of this new ruling class by insisting on the most extreme centralization of the economy. He wanted all the establishments of production and distribution to be part of that "single great enterprise which is the state," and claimed that "centralized planification is the way of life of socialist society, its definitive category" (Guevara, 1971c: 609).

To himself and to the world he justified his centralizing activity as the means to the creation of a new, socialist man, a human being purged of the original sin of acquisitiveness. In consequence, he demanded that "society in its entirety must convert itself into a gigantic school" (Guevara, 1971d: 631). One might add: a school with Fidel and himself as the teachers and the Cuban people as the pupils.

He grew restless in the unwanted role of administrator to which his false consciousness had led him. He left for a tour of the world, then went to the Congo to train guerrillas, and only returned to embark on his last, fateful adventure: the Bolivian expedition. The volunteers who accompanied him to Bolivia were former guerrillas who had become civilian and military bureaucrats, members of the ruling administrative class, among them a Vice-Minister of the Sugar Industry, a Director of Mines, a Chief of the Frontier Guards, and the Military Chief of a Province (Mallin, 1969: 229-231).

In a farewell letter to his parents, Che Guevara (1971a: 660) wrote on the eve of his departure for Bolivia: "Once again I feel the ribs of Rosinante under my heels; I return to the road with my leather shield strapped to my arm."

This was one of the frequent flashes of insight, of self-recognition, which made Guevara's personality so appealing in spite of his fanaticism. He was comparing himself to the supreme literary personification of false consciousness: Don Quijote de la Mancha, the impoverished small landowner steeped in the ideology of the medieval past, who imagined himself to be a knight errant and obstinately disregarded the counsel of the cynical realist as his elbow!

Che Guevara's life was dominated by the urge to self-sacrifice and, surely related to this, by a restlessness that caused him to roam through the Americas and later to take on official and unofficial missions to countries of four continents. Both traits manifested themselves long before he had become a guerrilla and a revolutionary. As an adolescent in the Argentinian city of Córdoba he had often visited a leprosarium in order to read to the patients. As a student, he had gone to Chile, hoping to find work in the leper-colony on the remote Chilean possession of Easter Island. When Easter Island proved inaccessible, he had traveled on to the Peruvian Amazon, where he worked for several months as a male nurse in the leprosarium of San Pablo (Rojo, 1969: 16-17). It was only later, after witnessing the CIA-staged overthrow of the reformist Arbenz government in Guatemala, that he decided to dedicate his life to revolution instead of tropical medicine.

The biographies of Latin American guerrilla activists would doubtless yield many instances of a similar spirit of abnegation and desire to serve humanity, coupled with a proclivity to violence that was certainly not foreign to Guevara himself. But this does not explain the peculiar social composition of the guerrilla movements. These movements express the despair of young members of the administrative class, radicalized and alienated from society by the deterioration of their prospects in countries of stagnant economy. In case of success, the movements offer political power and a new role for the administrative class: the administration of profound and worthwhile social change instead of mere paper-pushing in a deteriorating welfare-bureaucracy.

The political and ideological provenance of the membership of the Latin American urban guerrilla groups is heterogeneous: Stalinism, Maoism, Trotskyism, Castroism, Peronism. A strong contingent has been recruited from the ranks of the leftist, "Third-World Catholic" student movement. There is even a fascist strain. In the mid-1960s a group of Argentinian political exiles in Montevideo, members of the rightist-extremist, anti-Semitic Tacuara organization, collaborated with the incipient Tupamaro movement (Kohl and Litt, 1974: 186; Mercader and Vera, 1969: 87-93). After returning to Argentina, the Tacuara leader, Joe Baxter, is reported to have joined one of the two major urban guerrilla groups still operating in that country today, the ERP (Ejército Revolucionario del Pueblo), a group of Trotskyist origin, though now divorced from the various international factions of Trotskyism (Kohl and Litt, 1974: 330).

The other main Argentinian guerrilla group still active, the Montoneros, was founded in 1968 by Catholic and Peronist elements, but has since moved to "Marxist-Leninist" positions. In 1972 a Montonero spokesman, Fernando Vaca Narvaja, stressed the solidarity of his group with the liberation movements in other Latin American countries and declared the "strategic objective" of the Montoneros to be "to attain a socialist government in Argentina" (Kohl and Litt, 1974: 399).

The Brazilian guerrilla groups listed in Kohl and Litt's standard work on urban guerrilla warfare in Latin America had their origin either in secessions from the Brazilian Communist Party or in Trotskyism. All of them professed allegiance to "Marxism-Leninism."

The program for revolutionary social change issued by the Uruguayan Tupamaros in 1971 stressed the importance of "workers' administration"—not to be confused with self-management—of industrial and agricultural enterprises. This was probably a last remnant of the influence of their early mentor, the anarchist Abraham Guillén. Yet the same program insisted on the centralization of credit by the state, and the planning "in detail" of "production, commerce, credit and the economy in general" (Kohl and Litt, 1974: 293-294). It thus advocated the strengthening and expansion, not the destruction, of the state; anarchism is not and cannot be an ideology of the administrative class.

The Tupamaros professed an ostentatious pragmatism: "First came action, and then came theory" (Tupamaros, 1971: 36). However, Sir Geoffrey Jackson relates (1974: 68) that most of his captors were "straightforward Marxist-Leninist atheists." The one exception was a practicing Roman Catholic who "would not admit to being simultaneously a Marxist-Leninist, though he considered this a perfectly reasonable Third World Catholic position."

The "Marxism-Leninism" of the Latin American urban guerrillas is not the Marxism of Lenin, or the Marxism-Leninism of Stalin or even of Mao. It is the doctrine of the neo-Marxist dependency school that emerged in the late 1960s—a Marxism in essence reduced to an interpreation of the contemporary non-socialist world as a system of metropolis-satellite or center-periphery relations dominated by the multinational corporations.

The singleminded concentration on one subject—the policies and economics of imperialism—makes the neo-Marxist dependency theory acceptable to persons who would balk at the dialectical materialism of Marx, Engels, and Lenin on religious or philosophical grounds. That is what Sir Geoffrey Jackson's Catholic jailer meant when he claimed that "Marxism-Leninism," that is, the dependency theory, was "a perfectly reasonable Third World Catholic position."

The neo-Marxist dependency school's interpretation of imperialism differs greatly from Marx's and Lenin's view. In one of his essays on India, Karl Marx (1960: Vol 9: 220-226) maintained that England had a twofold mission in that country: "the destruction of the old Asian social order and the creation of the material conditions for a Western social order in Asia." He assumed that the construction of a railway system in India would lead to industrialization and modernization, thus creating the conditions for the expropriation of the means of production by the Indian people.

Lenin (1961: Vol. 1, 847-856) elaborated on this theme. In *Imperialism the Highest Stage of Capitalism* (1916) he approved the thesis of Hobson and Schultze-Gaevernitz that capital export would lead to the wholesale transfer of industries from Western Europe to the colonial and semicolonial countries. The latter would thus become industrialized, while the formerly highly industrialized countries would be transformed into "rentier states" inhabited by wealthy parasites living on the profits from overseas investments, and by a service class. According to Lenin, this unfortunate development could only be prevented by the European proletariat, which would have to rid itself of its reformist leaders in order to make the socialist revolution. And in his *Draft Theses on the National and Colonial question,* submitted to the Second Congress of the Comintern in 1920, Lenin (1961: Vol. 3, 492) postulated an alliance of the communist parties with the "bourgeois-democratic liberation movement" arising in the colonial and semicolonial countries as a result of their progressive industrialization.

In the same vein, Stalin (1952: Vol. 6: 66), in his *Foundations of Leninism* (1924) claimed that in exploiting the colonial and dependent countries, "imperialism is compelled to build there railways, factories and mills, industrial and commercial centers." This would lead to the awakening of national consciousness and the growth of the liberation movement, and would convert the colonies and dependent countries from "reserves of imperialism into reserves of the proletariat."

However, the industrialization of the backward countries was not proceeding at the pace envisaged by Marx and Lenin. In consequence, Stalin caused the Comintern quietly to replace Lenin's untenable thesis with a conspiracy theory according to which imperialism was deliberately sabotaging the industrialization of the colonial world in order to maintain it in the position of a provider of cheap raw materials and of a market for industrial goods. The Comintern claimed that imperialism was aided and abetted in this by allies within the exploited colonial and semicolonial countries: an oligarchy of feudal landowners and a "comprador bourgeoisie" of capitalists linked with the export-import trade. On the other hand, those capitalists who were struggling against the foreign monopolies in order to build up an industry catering to the internal market of the exploited countries formed a "national bourgeoisie" that was seen as an ally—though not a dependable one—of the proletariat and peasantry in the struggle against imperialism and feudalism. The aim of this triple alliance—proletariat-peasantry-national bourgeoisie—was an "anti-imperialist, anti-feudal, democratic revolution" that would prepare the way for the final, socialist revolution.

The message wrapped in this packet of doctrinaire Marxist-Leninist verbiage was one of moderation: the time for the socialist revolution has not yet come, and at this stage of the game the communists are still in need of "bourgeois" allies. Conscious of their weakness, the communist parties of Latin America held on to this convenient doctrine long after the demise of the Comintern and its successor, the Cominform. In the 1950s, at the height of the Latin American import-substitution industrialization drive, many non-Marxist Latin American political theorists also accepted the concept of a progressive, anti-imperialist "national bourgeoisie," and through them, this old Comintern formula even found its way into staid North American political science texts.

The communist party doctrine that conditions in Latin America were not yet ripe for a socialist revolution, and indeed the entire Leninist concept that socialism could only be brought about by revolutionary action of the proletariat led by its communist vanguard party, was refuted by life. The Cuban revolution showed that in Latin America it was possible for a small band of dedicated revolutionaries to come to power through rural guerrilla warfare, without the support of the urban proletariat, and then to implement a social revolution totally restructuring society from above, by administrative means.

The Cuban example had no immediate significant effect on the workers and peasants of other Latin American countries. In Chile the attempt of a radical labor leader, Clotario Blest, to lead the labor movement down the path of insurrection was easily thwarted by the communist party bosses. In Brazil, the Peasant Leagues, founded by a young patrician who had become a convert to Castroism, soon lost their impetus and disappeared without trace after the military coup of 1964.

On the other hand, the repercussions of the Cuban revolution in the upper sector of Latin American society were considerable. Throughout Latin America, the Cuban revolution gave birth to a militant New Left centered in the universities—several years before the emergence of similar movements of radicalized middle class youth in Europe and the United States.

Havana gave material and propagandistic support to the New Left revolutionaries, but failed to supply an adequate theoretical justification for armed struggle against the entire bourgeoisie, not just the "comprador bourgeoisie," and against democratic as well as dictatorial governments. Indeed, in his book, *Guerrilla Warfare* (1960), Che Guevara still maintained that guerrilla warfare was impossible in countries in which the appearance of democratic constitutional legality was maintained (see Guevara, 1971a: 27-28). In *The Second Declaration of Havana* (1962), a flaming call to arms, Fidel Castro declared the "national bourgeoisie" to be incapable of confronting Yankee imperialism (quoted in Guevara, 1971a: 553), and in his essay "Guerrilla Warfare—a Method" (1963), Guevara wrote that "the great majority of the national bourgeoisie have joined North American imperialism," (see Guevara, 1971a: 563) but these flat assertions were no substitute for analysis. Régis Debray's *Revolution in the Revolution?*, published in Havana in 1966, was merely an attempt to explain away the failure of previous guerrilla campaigns and to demonstrate that rural guerrilla warfare was still the correct road to power.

Trotskyist doctrine was too esoteric, and the Trotskyist movement too sectarian and rent by petty squabbles to appeal to more than a small minority of the Latin American New Left. The Maoist splinter parties, led by former communist party bureaucrats who were unrepentant Stalinists, were more interested in polemics against Moscow and the pro-Soviet communist parties than in promising revolution.

What the New Left revolutionaries needed was a theory that made it plausible that Latin America was ready for a socialist revolution in which there was no room for "national bourgeois" allies. The neo-Marxist dependency theory filled this need.

The neo-Marxist dependency theory was preceded, and at least in part inspired, by the so-called ECLA dependency theory first formulated by the Executive Secretary of the United Nations Economic Commission for Latin America (ECLA), Dr. Raul Prebisch, in his brochure *The Economic Development of Latin America and its Principal Problems* (United Nations, 1951).

According to Prebisch, the terms of trade between the underdeveloped, raw material producing countries of the periphery and the industrialized countries of the center favor the center: while the prices of industrial goods tend to remain stable or increase, those of raw materials fluctuate wildly with a long-run tendency to decline. Prebisch's original thesis was refined and somewhat amended in subsequent ECLA publications. In recent studies the worsening of the terms of trade of the underdeveloped countries is attributed largely to the oligopolistic organization of production and the power of the labor unions in the industrialized center: owing to this, increases in productivity through technological change and other factors result in rising wages and profits, but not in a decline in prices, while fierce competition among primary producers in the underdeveloped countries of the periphery forces their prices down. For the countries of the periphery, the obvious solution is the promotion of industrialization by the state through high tariffs and import restrictions, and through state investment in basic industries wherever private capital is lacking or unwilling to invest because of high risks and insufficient profits.

Ideology is ex post facto justification of policies. The ECLA dependency theory served to justify and speed up the import-substitution industrialization drive which in some Latin American countries had begun well over a decade before the theory was formulated. The neo-Marxist dependency theory justifying armed revolutionary struggle came into being in the late 1960s, at a time when rural guerrilla warfare was petering out after years of struggle, and the new stage of urban guerrilla warfare was beginning. As the Tupamaros put it: "first came action, practice, and then came theory."

As usual in Latin America, ideology was imported from abroad. The dependency theory originated in North America, among the circle of maverick Marxists clustered around Leo Huberman's and Paul Sweezy's *Monthly Review*. At the time, this publication, which today is in high repute as the most important and most serious theoretical organ of American neo-Marxism, was almost unknown in the United States, but its Spanish language edition, published in Buenos Aires and Santiago de Chile, was widely read and influential in Latin American leftist intellectual circles.

It was in the *Monthly Review* that a young political theorist of German origin, André Gunder Frank, published several of the essays in which he first outlined the fundamental theses of his theory of underdevelopment. The Latin American dependency theorists hesitate to acknowledge the full extent of their indebtedness to Frank, possibly because it is irksome to them that their interpretation of Latin American reality is of foreign origin.[4] In actual fact it was Frank who first elaborated, in full detail, the basic tenets of the dependency school. These are:

(1) The concept of the capitalist world as an all-encompassing, tightly knit system of center-periphery (or as Frank puts it, metropolis-satellite) relationships in which capital is concentrated in the centers, and the periphery is decapitalized on the local, national, regional, and global levels.

(2) As a consequence of this, the impossibility of independent economic development in the peripheral (satellite) countries. The only possible development in these countries is dependent development, which is tantamount to underdevelopment.

(3) Again as a consequence of this, the denial of the existence of a national bourgeoisie in the dependent (peripheral or satellite) countries. Since they are integrated into the world capitalist system of dependency relationships, the capitalists of these countries

cannot have independent national aims. They are agents of international monopoly capital who participate in the transfer of capital to the imperialist center (metropolis).

(4) From this it follows, at least for the more radical exponents of the dependency theory, that a peripheral (satellite) country can only achieve independent development by severing its economic and political ties with the capitalist world system, that is, by a socialist revolution.

Frank's first and most important book, *Capitalism and Underdevelopment in Latin America* (1967, augmented second edition in 1969) had an impact of well-nigh seismic proportions in Latin American intellectual circles. There followed a collection of essays, *Latin America: Underdevelopment or Revolution* (1969), which included a witty and often brilliant critique of North American theories of development. In *Lumpenbourgeoisie: Lumpendevelopment* (1972, first published in Spanish in 1970), Frank pilloried the Latin American capitalists as a *Lumpenbourgeoisie* serving the interests of "neo-imperialism."

In *Capitalism and Underdevelopment in Latin America* Frank (1969a: 9) develops the thesis that:

Economic development and underdevelopment are the opposite faces of the same coin. . . . One and the same historical process of the expansion and development of capitalism throughout the world has simultaneously generated—and continues to generate—both economic development and structural underdevelopment.

For Frank, underdevelopment is not a mere lack of or lag in development: it is the direct result of development. The development of the metropolis is achieved by decapitalization of the satellite; development at one pole causes underdevelopment at the other. In *Latin America: Underdevelopment or Revolution* (1969b: 4), he maintains that:

Even a modest acquaintance with history shows that underdevelopment is not original or traditional and that neither the past nor the present of the underdeveloped countries resembles in any important respect the past of the now developed countries. The now developed countries were never *under*developed though they may have been *un*developed.

Frank's thesis is that within the capitalist system, foreign investment does not and cannot benefit the host country. It is merely an instrument by which "economic surplus"[5] is sucked out of the satellite country and accumulated in the metropolis. And not only foreign investment generates underdevelopment. The satellization process continues within each satellite country: "economic surplus" is drawn out of rural areas which thus become underdeveloped, and drawn into industrialized regions which thus function as a local or national metropolis. It is in this context that Frank (1969a: 10) first enunciated the thesis that was to become the basic tenet of the entire dependency school:

> This contradictory metropolitan center—peripheral satellite relationship, like the process of surplus expropriation, runs through the entire world capitalist system in chain-like fashion from its uppermost world center, through each of the various national, regional, local and enterprise centers.

According to Frank (1972: 89), their class interest impels the Latin American capitalists to promote and increase the dependency and underdevelopment of their countries. This was true even in the 1930s and 1940s, when certain bourgeois governments attempted to implement "inward directed" development policies:

> The very "development" policy of the Latin American lumpenbourgeoisie proved to be an effective instrument of growing dependence and underdevelopment. In our own century as well, the class policy of the Latin American lumpenbourgeoisie has served the same purpose: while promoting neoimperialist development, it has fostered the even acuter neodependence and underdevelopment which characterize the present period.

Economic integration, the creation of a Latin American common market or free trade zone, is no defense against the exploitation and pauperization of the area. On the contrary, it would only increase exploitation of the masses by domestic and American capitalists:

> Given the present economic structure of Latin America, local capital is scarce; given the present political structure, foreign capital is "welcome". . . . Thus economic integration of Latin America under present circumstances will not only draw capital from the poor to the rich in Latin America itself. It will also make the poor Latin Americans poorer and the rich North Americans richer [Frank, 1969b].

Underdevelopment, in Frank's view, is not a phase or condition: it is a continuing process generated by the accumulation of "surplus" in the metropolis. He stresses again and again that the dependent, peripheral, or satellite countries can only escape this process by breaking out of the capitalist world system: "the only way out of Latin American underdevelopment is armed revolution leading to socialist development" (Frank, 1969a).

The Marxists believe in a historical law by which societies develop in a succession of stages. Feudalism, capitalism, and socialism are successive stages. Thus, a society cannot move directly from feudalism to socialism; it first has to pass through the capitalist stage. This is the basis of the orthodox Marxist-Leninist argument that Latin America is not yet ripe for the socialist revolution because there are still "feudal remnants" in its social system. Frank seeks to refute this argument by demonstrating that Latin America was never in the feudal stage, and this demonstration is, in the present author's view, the most impressive and convincing element in his entire theory.

Frank argues that the Spanish and Portuguese conquest of the area was an enterprise of early mercantilist capitalism, not of feudalism: it integrated the continent into the incipient world market by opening it up to exploitation of its natural resources and their transfer overseas. Frank is not alone in maintaining this. Before him, the Brazilian economic historians Roberto Simonsen (1962), a "bourgeois liberal" and Caio Prado (1965, 1963), a Marxist, had already conclusively documented the mercantilist nature of the Portuguese conquest of their country. Frank correctly argues that these findings also apply to the Spanish conquest. And if from the very beginning Latin America was not feudal, it follows logically that there cannot be "feudal remnants" in the area today.

Frank's view of the conquest as a capitalist enterprise opening up the newly discovered continent to exploitation of its resources for export overseas is indubitably correct; it is mere semantic quibbling if his orthodox Marxist-Leninist critics argue that it was a mercantilist and not a modern industrial capitalist enterprise. The new economic structure created by the Spanish and Portuguese conquerors was a mining and plantation economy producing for the overseas market. The colonial social structure developed from this economic base: the latifundia were founded in order to provide foodstuffs—grain and meat—for the export sector, that is, the mines, plantations, and port cities from which the export products were shipped overseas.

Frank points to Latin America's economic history to document his case. Cities and regions that were once the most developed in the area later sank into poverty and underdevelopment: Guanajuato in Mexico, Potosí in Bolivia; Minas Gerais in Brazil, after the mines were exhausted; the nitrate mining settlements of the northern desert in Chile became ghost towns after the invention of artificial nitrates in Germany; the Brazilian northeast was improverished by the decline of the sugar industry and the rubber capital of Manaus in the Amazon lost viability after the Malaysian plantations began to produce cheaper rubber. He stresses that manufacture or industry flourished briefly whenever world crisis or war interrupted the flow of trade with the European metropolis, only to decline and wither when trade was resumed. He concludes from this:

> no country that has been firmly tied to the metropolis as a satellite through incorporation into the world capitalist system has achieved the rank of an economically developed country, except by finally abandoning the capitalist system [Frank, 1969a: 11].

This apodictic statement disregards the cases of Canada, Australia, and New Zealand, countries whose wealth is based on the export of foodstuffs and raw materials and who achieved the rank of economically developed countries, although—or rather because—they were "firmly tied to the metropolis as satellites through incorporation into the world capitalist system." Moreover, Frank's presentation of Latin America's economic history is extremely one-sided. That history cannot be reduced to a mere succession of catastrophes and vain attempts to stave them off, to the exhaustion of mines and the collapse of nitrate or sugar prices.

As long as the Spanish invaders merely seized the gold and silver artifacts of the Aztecs, Mayas, Chibchas, and Incas, melted them down, and shipped them overseas, their activity was indeed purely destructive. But once mines and plantations went into production, new wealth was generated among the ruins of the old civilizations. Natural resources per se do not constitute wealth. They only become wealth when they are utilized, when the minerals are extracted, the forests hewn, the prairies planted or populated with cattle.

The architectural splendors of the Latin American cities, the glorious churches, palaces and mansions, parks and plazas all testify that part of the new wealth generated in the colonial era and the nineteenth century was not taken out, but remained in the area. It is true that the colonial governments, and in the nineteenth and early twentieth century Latin American governments, dominated by export-oriented agricultural and mining interests, stifled the growth of domestic manufacturing industries. But the ages of colonial mercantilism and nineteenth century free trade are long past. The process of industrialization in Latin America may be skewed and uneven, but it cannot be denied that it is taking place.

Like a lawyer arguing his case in court, Frank cites only those historical facts that he can use as evidence in support of his theory. But there are far worse flaws in his argument than the mere selective presentation of evidence. Thus, his writings contain many instances of primitive, prelogical thinking: he assumes that the value of a gift to the recipient is determined by the intentions of the donor. If these intentions are selfish, the gift must needs be useless or harmful.

For instance, Frank maintains that American aid and investment in Brazil are purely exploitative because they are "an instrument for obtaining considerable Brazilian riches and for preserving the present monopolist structure of the American economy." Alliance for Progress money is not aid, but "aid":

> Just as U.S. purchase of surplus agricultural products and their subsequent shipment abroad as "food for peace" supports the increasing monopolization and therefore excess capacity of U.S. agriculture, government "aid" money provides the credits for foreign purchase of increasingly monopolized U.S. industry [Frank, 1969: 153-154].

By Frank's logic or prelogic, "food for peace" shipments of American surplus agricultural products cannot help to stave off starvation because these shipments are in the interests of U.S. agricultural monopolies; Alliance for Progress aid cannot benefit Latin America because its purpose is to "improve conditions for American investment" (Frank, 1969b: 153). Indeed:

> Under the Alliance for Progress, especially, the emphasis of American public capital investment in Latin America is on education and health—latrine-building, as it has been aptly dubbed [Frank, 1969b: 151].

As for private foreign investment, it is harmful per se because its purpose is to yield a profit. What is more, to reinvest profits in the host country, or even to use depreciation charges for the renewal of equipment only increases exploitation and is thus even worse and more wicked than to take the profits and depreciation charges out of the country. Frank gives an instance from Canada:

> By 1964 ... the part of American investment in Canada that entered from the United States had declined to 5 percent, making the average American contribution of the total capital used by American firms in Canada during the period 1957-1964 only 15 percent. All the remainder of the "foreign investment" was raised in Canada through retained earnings (42 percent), depreciation charges (31 percent), and funds raised by American firms on the Canadian capital market (12 percent) ... There is reason to believe that this

American reliance on foreign capital to finance American "foreign investment" is still greater in the poor underdeveloped countries, which are weaker and more defenseless than Canada. This, then, is the source of the flow of capital on investment account from the poor underdeveloped countries to the rich developed ones [Frank, 1969a: 300-301].

As can be seen, Frank absurdly argues here that because Canada is strong, it can force the American investors to take at least part of their Canadian earnings and depreciation charges out of the country instead of reinvesting them on the spot; the poor underdeveloped countries, being weaker and more defenseless than Canada, have to tolerate the reinvestment of a far greater proportion of the earnings and depreciation charges of the foreign imperialist investors! In other words: investment per se is evil: it impoverishes those upon whom it is inflicted.

Nevertheless Frank also complains of insufficient American investment in Latin America. In a key passage in the chapter "Foreign Investment in Latin American Underdevelopment" of the second edition of his magnum opus, he compares the repatriated earnings from American holdings in the Third World with new American investments in that area, and finds the latter inadequate:

The conservative estimates of the United States Department of Commerce show that between 1950 and 1965 the total flow of capital on investment account from the United States to the rest of the world was $23.9 billion, while the corresponding capital inflow from profits was $37 billion, for a net inflow into the United States of $13.1 billion. Of these totals, $14.9 billion flowed from the United States to Europe and Canada while $11.4 billion flowed in the opposite direction, for a net outflow from the United States of $3.5 billion. Yet, between the United States and all other countries—that is, mainly the poor, undeveloped ones—the situation is reversed: $9.0 billion of investment flowed to these countries while $25.6 billion in profits flowed out of them, for a net inflow from the poor to the rich of $16.6 billion. The corresponding flow between the United States and Latin America was $3.8 billion from the United States to Latin America and $11.3 billion from Latin America to the United States, for a net outflow from Latin America to the United States of 7.5 billion [Frank, 1969a: 305-306].

These figures clearly show that in the period concerned American capitalists found it vastly more worthwhile to invest in Europe and Canada than in the rest of the world in general and in Latin America in particular: they invested $14.9 billion in Europe and Canada and only $3.8 billion in Latin America! Yet Frank somehow contrives to misinterpret the same data as signifying exactly the opposite: to him they show that between 1950 and 1965 investment in Latin America was much more profitable than investment in Europe and Canada.

On penetrating this fog of confusion and misinterpretation, one discovers behind it medieval ecclesiastical doctrine: the interdiction of profit-taking as usury. Frank postulates the correspondence of new investments to earnings from previous investments. To him, the repatriation of earnings from previous foreign investments is only justified if an equivalent amount is immediately returned in the form of new investment. In other words: American investment abroad must not be allowed to yield a net profit.

To phrase it even more succinctly, and taking into account Frank's concept of "internal satellization": his doctrine is that nothing may be taken out of an underdeveloped country, or of an area inside that country, or of a village inside that area, unless at least the equivalent sum is returned. If less than the equivalent is put back, the country, area, village is being robbed, becoming ever more underdeveloped and impoverished.

In other words, the notion of productive investment is foreign to Frank. In his view, capitalist investment does not increase output. It does not generate new wealth, but only transfers wealth that somehow, mysteriously, already existed, out of the hands of the producer into the hands of the investor. Frank's thesis is that within the capitalist system, one country's or one person's gain must necessarily be another's loss. Or to express it in the terminology of game theory: for Frank, capitalist investment is a zero-sum game.

This would of course be true if—and only if—the capitalist economy were one in which output is constant, in which a fixed quantity of wealth is constantly being produced and reproduced, distributed and redistributed. In such an economy development at one pole could indeed only be achieved by underdevelopment at the other pole, riches could only be accumulated by robbery, by the impoverishment of others.

The dependency school's theory of capitalist development and underdevelopment is based on this model of a totally stagnant, sterile economy.

How could Frank, an intelligent and even brilliant writer, commit such elementary mistakes in elaborating his dependency theory? And how could a theory based on misapprehensions, misinterpretations, and plain illogic spread like wildfire among the Latin American intelligentsia, converting so many economists, political scientists, sociologists, and historians that it quickly became the dominant school of thought at many Latin American universities?

The tenor of Frank's writings provides the key to the mystery. They are consistently on a high pitch of indignation and revulsion. His anger at an economic system based on profit-taking is so great as to render him uncritical: he immediately accepts any argument that is brought up against so vile a system, any data that at first glance seem to demonstrate its iniquity. The same note of moral indignation pervades the writings of his followers, the dependency school. These are not sober analyses but fiery denunciations resembling the sermons of the medieval clerics who inveighed against the sin of usury.

As Marxists, the dependency theorists hold that wealth is produced by the toilers in factories and fields, not by foreign investors or domestic capitalists; that private ownership of the means of production is parasitism; and that the responsibility for both production and distribution should be entrusted to selfless administrators working only for the good of the community, and not for personal gain. The Marxists claim to have demonstrated the inevitability of socialism, or at least its superior rationality, but their real argument is ethical, not economic; it is concerned with right and wrong, not with ways to increase output.

The opponents of Marxist revolutionary socialism are only able to counter this ethical condemnation of profit-taking with pragmatic arguments such as:

—Pure capitalism is a thing of the past; in the countries of the Western world, a large proportion of the economy is already under public ownership.

—Without the profit motive there would be no incentive for innovation and rationalization.

—However defective, the market mechanisms of capitalism are still cheaper and more efficient than the huge bureaucracy needed for the administration of a socialized economy.

—International economic relations based on magnanimity instead of self-interest may be theoretically feasible, but who can guarantee that in practice the administrative ruling class of a socialist country would generously defer surplus accumulation at home in order to speed the economic development of other countries? To take a purely hypothetical case: would the socialist government of the Soviet Union provide the means for the economic development of socialist China without demanding subservience as its price?

Such pragmatic arguments based on the superior efficiency of the capitalist system are unlikely to appeal to young Argentinians and Uruguayans who are being driven to desperation by their lack of prospects. And quite apart from this, there are historical factors, old traditions that render the denunciation of the profit motive as immoral particularly attractive to Latin American intellectuals of upper-class background.

V. THE VAMPIRE COMPLEX

In discussing the motivations of student radicals, Aldo Solari (1968: 96-97) points out that in demanding a socialist society, these radicals "are responding, to a great extent, to the influence of a system of traditional values." They reject the dependent capitalist society in which they are living, but "behind this rejection there lies hidden, to a good extent, . . . the attachment to the values of the traditional society with which they were raised . . . Behind the rejection of the values of capitalist industrial society . . . there is hidden the rejection of the values of any industrial society." Latin American student radicalism thus conforms to the usual pattern of generational conflict: the young do not rebel against the values inculcated in them by their elders, but against the compromises of the older generation, the seeming betrayal of these same values by their parents and teachers. The values to which Solari refers as those of "traditional society" are the Iberian aristocratic values of the Latin American upper sector.

André Gunder Frank's assertion that Latin America was never feudal, but capitalist from the very beginning, may well be true in the purely economic sphere. However it is beyond doubt that the Iberian rulers transplanted certain values and standards of medieval European society into the colonial upper class. First and foremost among these values was the ideal of the gentleman who does not soil his hands by handling coin in the marketplace. To this day in Latin America such professions as medicine, law, the arts, and administration, are the most respected. Trade and manufacturing are frequently left to upstarts from the lower classes, to Spanish, Portuguese, or Italian immigrants of peasant stock, and to Arabs, Hungarians, Chinese, and Jews. The successful businessman seeks to adapt to the aristocratic ideal: he buys a landed estate and raises his sons to become lawyers, doctors, architects; just as the English bourgeois does his utmost to conform to the English aristocratic standard of the gentleman.

The origins of the Latin American upper-sector values lie in the European medieval past, in a static economy in which the volume of agricultural production only fluctuated with the vagaries of the weather, and craftsmen produced manufactured goods to order, not for anonymous customers on the market. In such an economy one man's gain was necessarily another's loss. The medieval baron felt justified in preying on the wagontrains that passed by his castle, because he saw the merchant as a profiteer who sold more expensively than he bought. The baron knew only loans for conspicuous consumption—a wedding, a new coat of armor. The notion of a productive loan, of investment to increase output, was beyond him. He therefore hated and despised the dynamic elements in medieval society, the accumulators of capital. In his view, concentration of wealth at one pole could only be brought about by concentration of poverty at the other. The Church sanctified the baron's economic views by condemning the charging of interest as usury.

Marx defined ideology as false consciousness. It can also be defined as the secularization of religious concepts. Thus Marx and Engels saw the disintegration of primeval communistic society through the division of labor as mankind's Fall from Grace into alienation, and Frank's theory of underdevelopment through investment is a secularized version of the medieval Church doctrine on usury.

The impact of Frank's doctrine in Latin America can be gauged by the fact that the Latin American governments—representatives of the *Lumpenbourgeoisie,* to use Frank's own term—eagerly took it up as a demagogic argument in their efforts to obtain more American aid. On June 12, 1969, the foreign minister of Eduardo Frei's Chilean government, Gabriel Valdés, visited the White House in Washington as the officially designated spokesman for the foreign ministers of Latin America. On that occasion Valdés recapitulated Frank's thesis of capital drain through capital investment in the following terms:

> It is generally believed that our continent receives real financial aid. The data show the opposite. We can affirm that Latin America is making a contribution to financing the development of the United States and of other industrialized countries. Private investment has meant and does mean for Latin America that the sums taken out of our continent are several times higher than those that are invested. Our potential capital declines. The benefits of invested capital grow and multiply themselves enormously, though not in our countries but abroad. The so-called aid, with all its well-known conditions, means markets and greater development for the developed countries, but has not in fact managed to compensate for the money that leaves Latin America in payment of the external debt and as a result of the profits generated by private direct investment. In one word, we know that Latin America gives more than it receives. On these realities it is not possible to base any solidarity or even any stable or positive cooperation [quoted in Cockroft et al., 1972: IX; and in Frank, 1972: 94].

Latin American civilization is older than the Anglo-Saxon civilization of North America. Upper and middle-class Latin Americans are frequently more educated, and at least in some respects, more civilized than their counterparts in the United States. This makes the discrepancy in the levels of economic development all the more galling. Frank's doctrine provides an explanation of the discrepancy that is completely satisfying to the Latin American's self-esteem: Latin America's economic lag is not due to individual or collective failings, nor to an archaic, feudal social structure, nor, as the behaviorists claim, to a value-orientation that hampers economic growth. Latin America's lag is the direct result of North America's economic growth. Latin America is poor because the United States is rich!

In the circles that accept this doctrine, it produces a state of mind that can only be described as a collective psychosis—a vampire complex. The persons possessed by the vampire complex imagine the whole continent to be in the grip of a many-mouthed monster. The monster is imperialism, its present incarnation is the United States, and the multinational corporations are its mouths, sucking the lifeblood out of the countries of Latin America. The term "vampire complex" is entirely appropriate. There is even a book, by the Uruguayan writer Eduardo Galeano, which bears the significant title *Open Veins of Latin America*. The subtitle of the book is "Five Centuries of the Pillage of a Continent," and Galeano's thesis (1973: 12) is that of Frank:

> the winners happen to have won thanks to our losing: the history of Latin America is, as someone has said, an integral part of the history of world capitalism. Our defeat was always implicit in the victory of others; our wealth has always generated our poverty by nourishing the prosperity of others—the empires and their native overseers.

A psychosis is often logically structured: a series of logical conclusions built on a basic delusion. The psychosis may spread to normal persons and become collective if the basic delusion is not easily recognizable as such, and if known facts appear to support it. Many known facts can be cited in apparent support of the basic, fallacious assumption of the vampire complex.

It cannot be denied that the Spanish conquerors, in their quest for gold, destroyed the pre-Columbian civilizations. During the next three centuries, Iberian colonization was exploitative, even though it did build a new civilization. After the liberation from colonial rule, governments dominated by agrarian, mining, banking, and commercial interests adopted free-trade policies that stifled the growth of domestic industries.

Foreign investment has brought agricultural and industrial development, but the motives of the investors are not altruistic. Foreign companies seek to maximize profits. Their duty is to their shareholders, not to the country in which they invest. They have resorted to trickery, bribery, subversion; and they have encouraged coups in order to obtain contracts detrimental to the host country. Whenever possible, they enlist the aid of their own governments to exert diplomatic pressure.

Development in Latin America is indeed lopsided. It fails to benefit the rural masses and is responsible for the squalor of the big-city slums and shanty-towns. Latin America is far more in need of mass transportation systems, clean drinking water, and paramedics for the villages than of private automobiles, Coca Cola plants, and heart specialists for plutocrats.[6] Unfortunately, not only the Latin American plutocrats, but also the politically decisive middle classes and even the workers desire the American way of life. The white-collar employee aspires to an automobile, the blue-collar worker to a refrigerator, and the shanty-town inhabitant to a television set. It would probably take a totalitarian regime of the Chinese or Cuban type to change the direction of investment by imposing austerity. Once such a dictatorship is established, it is difficult to get rid of it after it has fulfilled its task. As a great Mexican statesman and soldier, General Alvaro Obregón, once put it (quoted in Blanco, 1967: II, 295):

"The three great enemies of the Mexican people are militarism, clericalism and capitalism. We [the military] can get rid of capitalism and clericalism, but who will then get rid of us?"

Multinational corporations avoid or decrease taxation of the profits of their subsidiaries abroad by charging them exaggerated prices for supplies imported from company-owned establishments elsewhere; the profits are thus transferred abroad by a simple bookkeeping operation. The interests of foreign mining companies often conflict with those of the host countries. Ores are shipped abroad because it is not in the interests of the company to build processing plants near the mines. Reserves remain untapped; production in Latin America has been restricted in order to sustain marginally profitable mines in the United States.

U.S. foreign aid opens new markets to American industry because its recipients are obliged to use it for the acquisition of American goods. European-built power stations and other electrical equipment—even the machinery-driven elevators in office and apartment buildings—are rendered obsolete and have to be replaced because they do not conform to the standards of the American equipment acquired with U.S. aid funds.

U.S. economic and military aid is given in order to strengthen the hand of America's friends in Latin America. It bolsters governments against their opposition, thus preserving the status quo. The Public Safety Program of the U.S. government's foreign aid agency, USAID, provides advisors to Latin American police forces—a provision imposed on the reluctant agency by Act of Congress. The Pentagon gives counterinsurgency training to the armed forces of Latin American countries. American financial aid is given to anticommunist trade unions, cultural organizations, and political parties. The year 1965 saw the revival of the old policy, abandoned by President Franklin D. Roosevelt, of sending the Marines to the Caribbean.

In execution of the policies of four successive presidents, the Central Intelligence Agency has sought to control political life in the Latin American countries. In 1954 it organized the overthrow by force of the elected president of Guatemala. In 1961 it attempted to overthrow the Castro government in Cuba by a military force of exiles it had trained and equipped. From 1970 to 1973 it financed a "destabilization" campaign against the government of Chile that resulted in the overthrow and death of President Allende. Schemes to assassinate Fidel Castro were hatched by the CIA. The full story of the CIA's involvement in the overthrow of President Goulart of Brazil may never be revealed; and the story of its involvement in the assassinations of the mad dictator Trujillo in the Dominican Republic and of the commanding officer of the Chilean army, General Schneider, is only now emerging.

The above paragraphs may contain a one-sided account of foreign and specifically American economic and political activities in Latin America, but it cannot be denied that this account is based on fact. In itself, a one-sided presentation of facts does not constitute psychosis. It becomes psychotic only when presented as evidence in support of the fallacious thesis upon which the entire structure of mad logic is built.

The vampire complex is based on the fallacy or delusion that investment does not generate wealth, but only transfers it, thus depriving the former possessor of the capital needed for his own development and condemning him to underdevelopment and impoverishment. None of the facts cited above constitutes proof of this thesis, but the impressive recital of all the past and present misdeeds of imperialism and big business serves as a deterrent to critical examination of the thesis. Even those who are too skeptical to accept the fallacy as truth will often tend to regard it merely as an exaggerated conclusion drawn from solid facts and sound premises. They will fail to recognize it as the delusion at the root of a dangerous psychosis.

Once the basic fallacy is accepted, logic becomes madness. If foreign investment causes underdevelopment and impoverishment, any government permitting such investment is consciously or unconsciously a government of traitors, enriching other countries at the expense of its own. The same applies to all those who collaborate in any way with foreign investors—that is, the entire indigenous Latin American capitalist class—the *Lumpenbourgeoisie*. Since the industrial workers are those who most directly suffer from exploitation by foreign and domestic investors, it is assumed that they can easily be jolted into revolt by the armed action of a determined minority, an "insurrectionary nucleus." That is the reasoning of the Latin American urban guerrilla groups.

In a further stage of the psychosis, organized labor is seen as a "labor aristocracy" corrupted by the system. This accusation has been leveled against the Chilean socialist and communist workers by leftist intellectuals in whose view they displayed insufficient revolutionary ardor in the period of Salvador Allende's presidency.

There then remain, as the only class with true revolutionary potential, the subproletariat of the shanty-towns and the agricultural laborers. If they also fail to respond to the call to arms, it must be because they are still—to quote the arrogant paternalistic words of the Brazilian educator Paulo Freire (1971: 94-95)— "lacking in critical understanding of their reality." If the peasants of southeastern Bolivía did not support Che Guevara, it was not because their common sense made them aware of the folly of his enterprise, nor because in that empty region, there was no land-hunger to drive them to desperation. No: "The internalization of the oppressor by the dominated consciousness of the peasants explains their fear and their inefficiency" (Freire, 1971: 166).

The French bourgeois revolutionaries of 1789 humbly listened to the complaints of workers and peasants, took them down in their notebooks, the *cahiers de doléance,* and presented them to the National Assembly. On the other hand, today in Latin America, young members of the administrative class, themselves imbued with the false consciousness of being the repositories of proletarian class-spirit, go to shanty-towns and rural hovels in order to engage the inhabitants in a Socratic dialogue through which they will be "awakened to critical consciousness," and taught to reflect, because "reflection—true reflection—leads to action" (Freire, 1971: 52). In other words, the poorest of the poor are to be persuaded to sacrifice their lives for a revolution that will bring total power to the administrative class.

The Latin American vampire complex is in some ways reminiscent of the suffocation complex that befell a part of the German nation in the period between the world wars. The victims of this complex believed that a conspiracy of foreign governments and German traitors was suffocating the German people by depriving them of *Lebensraum*—living space. They held that this conspiracy had brought about the world war, in which the German armies had held their own until stabbed in the back by a revolution instigated by Judaeo-Marxism. From this point onward—the acceptance of the "stab-in-the-back" myth—logic became madness. Nevertheless, during an entire decade only a relatively small minority succumbed to the suffocation complex. It was only in the atmosphere of despair created by the Depression that the psychosis spread enough to bring the Nazis to power.

History cured the German psychosis by shock-treatment. Germany lost a second war in such a manner as to make it impossible for the military to claim that they had been stabbed in the back. On the contrary, the magnitude of the disaster was obviously due to the excessive loyalty of too many military men to an inept leader. Defeat inflicted far greater territorial losses in World War II than in World War I, and the population of Western Germany was swollen by the influx of many millions of refugees. Then came the German economic miracle. More Germans experienced greater affluence than ever before. The thesis that the German nation was being suffocated by lack of living space was revealed as patently absurd. The suffocation complex was dispelled. It now appears that history may also dispel the Latin American vampire complex—and in an infinitely less painful manner.

No group of men had been more hated and reviled by the Latin American extreme left than the leaders of Acción Democrática, the major populist party of Venezuela. These men were incessantly denounced as puppets of Yankee imperialism, stooges of the oil companies, contemptible traitors who were permitting the depletion of Venezuela's natural resources. The year 1973 has revealed that they are anything but puppets or traitors. They had been prime movers in the formation of OPEC, the cartel of oil-producing countries, thus demonstrating in the most convincing manner their ability and determination to promote the interests of their country in defiance of the United States. The same was achieved by the military rulers of a far smaller and less-developed country that has often been shrugged off as a mere "banana republic"—Ecuador.

Besides bringing personal vindication to a number of Latin American political leaders, OPEC demonstrated an important principle. The Marxists, and many non-Marxists as well, had hitherto taken it for granted that ownership is practically synonymous with control. Yet the oil companies, immensely wealthy international monopolies, have been unable to set the price of their own products. A closely related assumption has also been proved fallacious: the assumption that foreign ownership of the major industries of a country necessarily means foreign control of that country's government. The oil companies cannot prevent the nationalization of their property by states whose budgets and total assets are several times smaller than their own.

The same year 1973 also saw an event from which many have drawn a very different conclusion: the overthrow and death of Salvador Allende. Yet the concerted efforts of the CIA, powerful multinational corporations, and the Chilean right had failed to prevent the assumption of power by Allende. Nor had the armed forces moved against him when he confiscated the holdings of the American mining companies in Chile, nor when the leading Chilean industrial and financial establishments were socialized. The Chilean tragedy merely proved that it is unwise for a government not in complete control of its armed forces simultaneously to defy .the strongest power of the Hemisphere and the politically decisive sector of its own population—the middle classes, not the oligarchy.

The success of OPEC, on the other hand, shows that it is possible for small, weak, and underdeveloped countries to assert their independence without the fulfillment of André Gunder Frank's postulate (1969a: 277):

"the destruction of the capitalist structure itself and . . . liberation from the world imperialist-capitalist system as a whole . . ."

It has been argued that the cases of Venezuela and Ecuador are completely atypical and accidental because these countries produce and export such a vitally important resource as oil. It is also possible, and even likely, that the development of alternative energy sources will force oil prices down. But even if the OPEC cartel should collapse entirely, the oil companies would not recover their holdings which have been nationalized. Furthermore, the world demand for other natural resources exported from Latin America is also rising. The prices of these products fluctuate, but their overall upward trend is undeniable. The era in which countries dependent on the export of primary products are disadvantaged and condemned to underdevelopment is apparently drawing to a close.

This holds true for agricultural even more than for mineral resources. Sir Geoffrey Jackson relates (1974: 183) that in one of his discussions with his captors he asked them:

> to consider the possibility that Uruguayan beef was an indefinitely renewable raw material, not an exhaustible mineral the reserves of which could be depleted. To the contrary, my thesis was that good husbandry, and the best foreign cooperation could actually increase that resource. But such a possibility ran straight across doctrines of neo-imperialism and class-struggle; so a promisingly juicy argument ran out into the sand.

That was in 1971. Since then, it has become increasingly difficult to deny that agricultural exports may benefit a country and provide the means for its general economic development.

Doctrinaire Marxists interpret events such as the formation of OPEC and the rising prices of raw materials as manifestations of crisis brought about by the ever-deepening contradictions within the world capitalist system, and deduce from this that the moment of its collapse is near.[7] Others maintain that the capitalist system can adapt to such changes, even to such a catastrophe as the military and political defeat of the major capitalist power in Vietnam. They point out that, inexplicably for the Marxists, capitalist production has continued to rise, and capitalism continues to generate technological innovation, even though the geographical area in which the capitalist system holds sway has greatly diminished. Only history can render the final verdict in this dispute.

VI. CONCLUSIONS

The social base of the contemporary Latin American terrorist movements is constituted by the youth of the administrative class: educated persons without independent means and in need of administrative employment. Support for terrorism depends on the degree to which this class is driven to frustration and despair by its living conditions.

Yet terrorism in Latin America cannot be explained as a mere manifestation of demoralization and despair, a mere symptom of economic stagnation and social putrefaction. On the contrary, it is a vigorous reaction against this stagnation and putrefaction by the most energetic members of the administrative class, a bid for absolute power in order to give that class the challenging task of totally transforming society.

In Chapter II we quoted the Brazilian economic historian Caio Prado Junior's observation that from the 1930s onward there came into being in his country "around the state administration a dense network of private businesses directly or indirectly promoted by and maintained at the expense of the state."

"Bureaucratic capitalism" is Caio Prado's (1966: 195) name for this "hybrid sector in which public and private transactions are intertwined and intimately linked" (Prado, 1966: 193). Both partners benefit by this symbiotic relationship, which came into being through the import-substitution drive. High tariff walls favor domestic industry and trade at the expense of agriculture and the old, established import trade. The state apparatus derives licit revenues by taxation of this new private sector, and individual bureaucrats derive illicit gains through graft and other forms of corruption. Employment opportunities for the sons and daughters of bureaucrats, businessmen, and professionals are generated in private enterprise, the steadily expanding state bureaucracy, and the new parastatal enterprises.

In the words of Caio Prado (1966: 192), institutionalized corruption, "the more or less illicit enrichment of private individuals at the expense of and through the offices of the state . . . becomes a system playing a major role in the entire economy of the country, . . . a veritable economic category and specific form of large-scale capitalist accumulation." This applies not only to Brazil but also, and perhaps even more so, to such bastions of "bureaucratic capitalism" as Mexico and Venezuela.

Paradoxically this utterly corrupt system facilitates political stability. It diminishes tensions by rendering the rotation of power within the political elite less painful. The availability of lucrative employment in the private sector makes it easier for the members of a government and their personal clienteles to relinquish office, and less urgent for competing parties, or rival cliques within the ruling party, to seek power by fair means or foul.

However, the system only functions in a flourishing economy with a dynamic, expanding private sector. In times of recession or stagnation, private enterprise, the junior partner in the symbiotic relationship, can no longer fulfill its licit and illicit obligations to the state bureaucracy. The flow of both tax money and bribes diminishes, and there are fewer alternative employment opportunities to offer to politicians and their clienteles. It is at this point that desperation and revolt become rife among the youth of the administrative class, who are now faced with the prospect of unsatisfactory employment in a deteriorating environment, if not of actual unemployment.

Brute force can suppress terrorism, but it cannot eliminate the root of the evil: stagnation and decay of the economy causing the

living standard in the middle income brackets to fall and demoralization and putrefaction to spread in the upper sector of the
afflicted society. Our "social engineers" tell us that a numerous
middle class is the prerequisite for democracy and political stability. But what if the economic base of this "middle class" is
unhealthy: an industry with inadequate markets that can only be
maintained behind the shelter of high tariff walls and that demands excessive imports of raw materials and machinery? In that
case the industry consumes more wealth than it produces; balance
of payments deficits, rampant inflation, and declining living standards are the results.

It is no mere coincidence that today the three most troubled
countries of the Hemisphere are those of the Southern Cone:
Argentina, Chile, and Uruguay. These are countries with literacy
rates of 90 or more percent and an upper sector that includes a
numerous dependent and self-employed "middle class." In all
three countries a large domestic industrial sector is maintained at
the expense of the export sector. In spite of the considerable rise
in world market prices for minerals, wheat, and meat that has
taken place in the course of the last decade, the export sector—
mining in Chile, agriculture in Argentina and Uruguay—is no
longer able to pay the cost of the vast bureaucracy and the
inefficient domestic industries.

One solution would be a revolution leading to the installation
of a Cuban-style dictatorship. The private sector would then be
expropriated, the owners and administrative personnel would be
demoted to menial positions on the lowest rungs of the administrative ladder, or forced to emigrate. The trade unions would
cease to be an independent force, and the new ruling elite would
then be free to follow Fidel Castro's example in switching all
available resources to the export sector—the traditional source of
wealth in all the countries of Latin America.

Today, the only feasible alternative to this revolutionary solution would appear to be a shrinkage of the state apparatus
through dismissals and of the private sector through bankruptcies,
leading to white-collar and academic unemployment as well as
unemployment in the lower sector, and through this, to the

actual proletarization of a part of the upper sector. This extra-ordinarily painful procedure, never before undertaken in Latin America, can only be implemented by a brutal military dictator-ship. That is the road now taken by the government of Chile and also, apparently, of Uruguay. In Argentina, a country with a far larger internal market and a greater economic potential, adjust-ment would be less painful, but it is blocked by a powerful trade union movement that the military is reluctant, and possibly unable, to confront.

The course of history cannot be predicted; it is too often determined by chance and circumstance. Economic changes or failures of leadership may lead other Latin American nations into the morass in which the nations of the Southern Cone are foundering. Favorable changes are equally unpredictable. At the time of its formation in 1960, who would have foretold the spectacular success of OPEC and the resultant rise of Venezuela to a position of leadership in Latin America?

The attempts of political scientists to construct a compu-terized crystal ball in which to see the future are as vain as the attempts of the ancient alchemists to convert base metal into gold. Political scientists can at best reach tentative explanations of current political phenomena by sober examination of the available relevant facts. That is what we have attempted to do in this study of the phenomenon of terrorism in Latin America.

NOTES

1. See British Ambassador Jackson's description of his own kidnapping in his book (1974).

2. A similar claim had already been made in 1963 by the Peruvian Trotskyist Hugo Blanco, who asserted that he had managed to establish a parallel revolutionary power in two Andean valleys. However, his claim was based on a misreading of Trotsky's *History of the Russian Revolution,* which indeed refers to the existence of dual powers in the "prerevolutionary period" in Russia. However, it is clear from the passage cited by Blanco that what Trotsky had in mind was the period between the collapse of Czarist state authority in March 1917 and the seizure of power by the Bolsheviks in November of that year (see Blanco, 1972: 53-54). During these eight months the revolutionary parallel power of the Soviets existed openly side by side with the old state power, which was unable to suppress it. The armed peasant unions organized by Hugo Blanco in the Andean valleys of Convención and Lara did not constitute such a parallel power. They were a purely local organization easily suppressed by the government once it decided to move in the troops.

3. Foster (1924) attributes the revolutionary turmoil in the Mexico of his time exclusively to the need of the *caudillo* to dispense patronage in a society in which personal loyalty is the supreme value. He points out that "it is only a comparatively small part of the population that follows [the caudillo]. The great majority of the Mexican people *are* peaceable; they are tired of revolution; they have lost faith in new leaders; they prefer to remain neutral, and to cheer diplomatically for whoever proves the victor" (Foster, 1924: 184).

4. In an American publication, Fann and Hodges (1971: 179 ft.), Susanne Bodenheimer lists as representatives of the dependency school: Theotonio dos Santos, Fernando Cardoso, Enzo, Faletto, Aníbal Quijano, Osvaldo Sunkel, José Luís Reyna, Edelberto Torres, Tomás Vasconi, Marcos Kaplan, Pablo González-Casanova, and Dale Johnson. She sees Frank as a mere "predecessor," though admitting that the dependency theorists "incorporated some of the principal theoretical contributions of André Gunder Frank's analysis of underdevelopment."

5. Frank attributes the authorship of the concept of economic surplus to his mentor, the Marxist economist Paul Baran. In his book *The Political Economy of Growth,* Baran (1957) defines economic surplus as that part of total output which is either actually or potentially available for the accumulation of capital, that is, the formation of new, additional capital. Frank uses the term economic surplus much more loosely. He indiscriminately employs it as a synonym for profits, for capital per se, and for both at the same time. He does not bother with fine distinctions between profits

that are consumed and profits that are accumulated, or between capital needed to keep production going on the same scale as before, and new capital used to increase production.

6. This is the "Third World Catholic" criticism of Latin American development as stated in Illich (1971: ch.ll).

7. This is also André Gunder Frank's explanation. In an article (1974) he states that: "The evidence is accumulating that 'dependence'—both old and new—has ended or is completing that cycle of its natural life at least in the Latin America that gave it birth. The reason is the crisis of the 1970s in the newly changing world economic and political reality." In other words: if reality contradicts the dependency theory, that does not constitute a crisis of the theory, but a crisis of reality.

REFERENCES

BARAN, P. (1957) The Political Economy of Growth. New York: Monthly Review Press.

BLANCO, H. (1972) Land or Death, the Peasant Struggle in Perú. New York: Pathfinder Press.

BLANCO Moheno, R. (1967) Crónica de la Revolución Mexicana, tomo II. Mexico: Editorial Diana.

CARDILLO, L. M. (1975) The Tupamaros: A Case of Power Duality in Uruguayan Politics. Manuscript on deposit at Fletcher School of Law and Diplomacy, Tufts University, Medford, Massachusetts.

COCKROFT, J. et al. (1972) Dependence and Underdevelopment, Latin America's Political Economy. New York: Anchor.

COHEN, B. J. (1973) The Question of Imperialism. New York: Basic Books.

DEBRAY, R. (1967) Revolution on the Revolution. New York: Monthly Review Press.

FERNANDEZ, J. A. (1970) The Political Elite in Argentina. New York: N.Y. Univ. Press.

FANN, K. and D. HODGES (eds.) (1971) Readings in U.S. Imperialism. Boston: Porter Sargent.

FORTOUL, G. (1947) Historia Constitucional de Venezuela, Vol. III. Caracas: Editorial Novedades.

FOSTER, H. L. (1924) A Gringo in Mañanaland. New York: Dodd, Mead.

FRANK, A. G. (1974) Article in Latin American Perspectives (Spring): Vol. I, NO. 1.

–––(1972) Lumpenbourgeoisie, Lumpendevelopment. New York: Monthly Review Press.

–––(1969a) Capitalism and Underdevelopment in Latin America (sec. ed.). New York: Monthly Review Press.

––– (1969b) Latin America: Underdevelopment or Revolution. New York: Monthly Review Press.

FREIRE, P. (1971) Pedagogy of the Oppressed. New York: Herder & Herder.

GALEANO, E. (1973) Open Veins of Latin America, Five Centuries of the Pillage of a Continent. New York: Monthly Review Press.

GILLO, M. E. (1970) The Tupamaro Guerrillas. New York: Ballantine.

GUEVARA, E. C. (1971a) Obra Revolucionaria. Mexico: Ediciones Era (fourth ed.).

––– (1971b) "La guerra de guerrillas." in Guevara (1971a).

––– (1971c) "La planificación socialista, au significado." in Guevara (1971a).

––– (1971d) "El socialismo y el hombre en Cuba." in Guevara (1971a).

HODGES, D. C. [ed.] (1973) Philosphy of the Urban Guerrilla, the Revolutionary Writings of Abraham Guillén. New York: William Morrow.

ILLICH, I. (1971) Celebration of Awareness. Garden City, New York: Anchor Books.

JACKSON, Sir G. (1974) Surviving the Long Night. New York: Vanguard.

KIRKPATRICK, J. (1971) Leader and Vanguard in Mass Society: A Study of Peronist Argentina. Cambridge: M.I.T. Press.

KOHL, J. and J. LITT (1974) Urban Guerrilla Warfare in Latin America. Cambridge: M.I.T. Press.

Latin America (1970-1975) Newsletters. London.

LENIN, V. I. (1961) Ausgewaehlte Werke (vols. 1 and 3). Berlin: Dietz.

LIEBMAN, A. et al. (1972) Latin American University Students, a Six Nation Study. Cambridge: Harvard Univ. Press.

MARX, K. and F. ENGELS (1960) Werke (vol. 9). Berlin: Dietz.

MALDONADO, D. M. (1971) Puerto Rico, una Interpretacíon Histórico-Social. Mexico: Siglo Veintuno Editores (fourth ed.).

MALLIN, J. [ed.] (1971) Terror and Urban Guerrillas, A Study of Tactics and Documents. Coral Gables: Univ. of Miami Press.

——— [ed.] (1969) "Che" Guevara on Revolution. Coral Gables: Univ. of Miami Press.

MARTINS Rodrigues, L. (1966) Conflito Industrial e Sindicalismo no Brasil. São Paulo: Difusão Européia do Livro.

MERCADER, A. and J. de VERA (1969) Tupamaros: Estrategia y Accíon. Montevideo: Editorial Alfa.

Military Review, Ft. Leavenworth (1973) vol. LIII, no. 4 (April).

MOSS, R. (1972) The War for the Cities. New York: Coward, McCann.

d'OLIVIERA, COL. S. L. (1973) "Uruguary and the Tupamaro Myth." Military Review (April).

PORZECANSKI, A. C. (1973) Uruguay's Tupamaros, The Urban Guerrilla. New York: Praeger.

PRADO Junior, C. (1966) A Revolucão Brasileira. São Paulo: Editôra Brasilense.

——— (1965) História Econômica do Brasil. São Paulo: Brasiliense (ninth ed.).

——— (1963) Formacao do Brasil Contemporaneo. São Paulo: Brasiljense (seventh ed.).

PREBISCH, Raul (1951) The Economic Development of Latin America and its Principal Problems, United Nations.

ROJO, R. (1969) My Friend Che. New York: Dial.

SIMONSEN, R. C. (1962) História Econômica do Brasil. São Paulo: Companhia Editora Nacional (fourth ed.).

SOLARI, A. E. (1968) Estudiantes y Politica en América Latina. Caracas: Monte Avila Editores.

STALIN, J. W. (1952) Werke (volume 6) Berlin: Dietz.
TUPAMAROS (1971) Actas Tupamaras. Buenos Aires: Schapire.
UNESCO (1973) Yearbook.
––– (1963) Yearbook.

Subscribers to *The Washington Papers* are entitled to a special 20 percent discount on all of the following CSIS publications. Orders must refer to *Washington Paper* subscription to qualify and be prepaid to: Georgetown Center for Strategic and International Studies, 1800 K St. NW, Washington, DC 20006.

The 1975 CSIS Quadrangular (Quad II) Conference:	List Price	Discount Price
1. **Interrelationship of Inflation/Recession, the International Financial Structure, and Alliance Security,** rapporteur E. Luttwak (1975); 63 pp.,	$3.95	$3.15
2. **Commissioned Papers on Inflation/Recession—Quad II,** H. Block and H. Johnson (1975); 66 pp.,	$5.00	$4.00
3. **Selected Papers on Inflation/Recession—Quad II,** ed. by P. Hartland-Thunberg (1975); 156 pp.,	$5.00	$4.00
4. **International Information, Education, and Cultural Relations: Recommendations for the Future,** panel with F. Stanton et al. (1975); 96 pp.,	$3.95	$3.15
5. **Soviet-United States Naval Balance,** R. Kilmarx (1975); 187 pp.,	$5.00	$4.00
6. **Western World under Economic Stress,** P. Hartland-Thunberg (1975); 14 pp.,	$1.50	$1.20
7. **The Soviet Union and the Western Crisis,** W. Laqueur et al. (1975); 31 pp.,	$4.00	$3.15
8. **Freedom in the Third World,** T. Sumberg (1975); 91 pp.,	$5.00	$4.00
9. **The Economic Prospects of the Persian Gulf Amirates,** F. K. Lundy (1974); 95 pp.,	$5.00	$4.00
10. **The International Relations of Southern Africa,** ed. by C. Crocker (1974); 113 pp.,	$2.50	$2.00
11. **Commercial Diplomacy,** by L. Barrows (1974); 128 pp.,	$5.00	$4.00

Special 20 percent discount on CSIS publications to all

Washington Paper
subscribers